P9-DEK-298

Childcraft

THE HOW AND WHY LIBRARY

VOLUME 5

About Animals

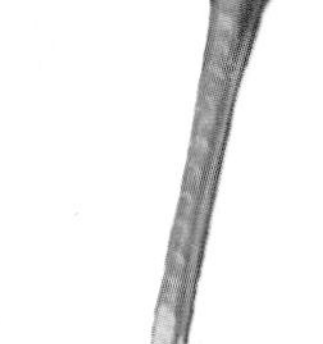

World Book, Inc.

a Scott Fetzer company

Chicago London Sydney Toronto

Childcraft—The How and Why Library
(Reg. U.S. Pat. and T.M. Off.—Marca Registrada)

World Book, Inc.
525 W. Monroe
Chicago, IL 60661

ISBN 0-7166-0193-1
Library of Congress Catalog Card Number 92-64103
Printed in the United States of America
B/IB

Acknowledgments

The publishers of *Childcraft—The How and Why Library* gratefully acknowledge the courtesy of the following publishers and organizations. Full illustration acknowledgments for this volume appear on pages 296-297.

Page 261: Reproduction of painting by Don Richard Eckelberry, © Frame House Gallery, Louisville, Ky.

Volume 5

About Animals

Contents

A sea gull is an animal.

The Animal Kingdom

What's the difference between a pussy willow and a pussycat?

For a pussy willow, being alive is growing from a seed in the ground. It is having roots to get water from the ground. It is staying in one place, for pussy willows can't move around. It is having green leaves that take in the summer sunlight and use it to make food. It is having seeds from which new pussy willows may grow.

That's the way of pussy willows. They are plants.

For a pussycat, being alive is being born, and eating, and growing. It is moving around. It is learning about other animals, and playing and making noises. It is growing up and having little kittens.

That's the way of pussycats. They are animals.

A red fox is an animal.

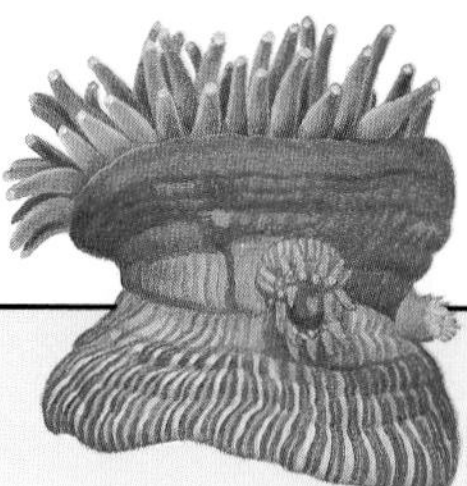

A sea anemone is an animal.

A kitten is an animal.

Banded Anemone

Is this a flower eating a fish? No, this is an animal called a sea anemone eating a fish.

Plant or animal?

Do you know the best way to tell the difference between a plant and an animal? You can't always tell by just looking. Some plants look like animals and some animals look like plants.

At the bottom of the sea, there is a living thing that looks like a flower growing out of the sand. But if a fish swims by and touches the "flower's" petals, the fish gets caught. A little mouth opens up in the middle of the "flower" and into it goes the fish!

Do plants have mouths? Can they eat things?

No. No plant in the world has a mouth. And most green plants make their own food from sunshine, air, and water. But animals can't make their food. They must eat.

Now the "flower" on the sea bottom moves. It slides slowly over the sand. Can a plant move?

No. Once a plant sprouts up from its seed it stays in the same place unless it is moved by man, an animal, or the wind. But most animals can move by themselves.

So this living thing at the bottom of the sea is not a plant, because it moves and eats. It is an animal called a sea anemone.

If a living thing moves about and eats, it is an animal.

Animals move

Plants can't move from place to place by themselves, but animals move in many different ways.

A clam has one foot that it uses for digging into mud or sand.

A penguin walks on two legs.

A kudu walks or runs on four legs.

Ladybugs walk on six legs.

Spiders walk on eight legs.

Centipedes may have a hundred pairs of legs on which to walk, and some millipedes walk on more legs than that.

Snakes slide on no legs at all.

Bats and many kinds of birds and insects fly. Fish swim.

Some animals move only when they are young. Barnacles, sponges, and baby oysters swim through the water until they find a good place to stay. Then they fasten themselves down and never move again.

Animals can move around without help. If it moves by itself, it's an animal.

Centipede

A centipede is an animal that moves on many legs. This centipede has forty legs. Some centipedes have more.

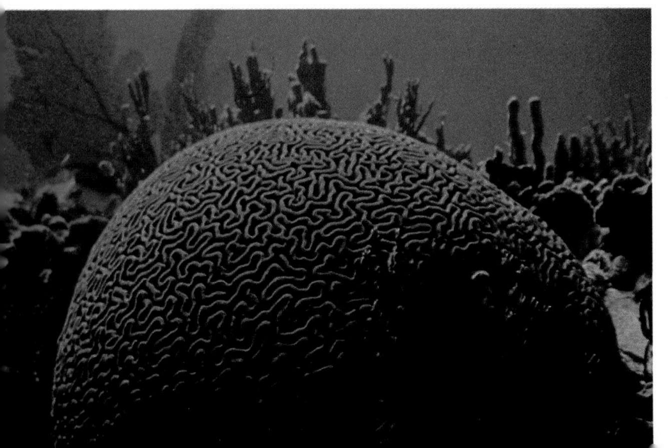

Little wormlike animals live inside these twisty tunnels. They poke their heads up, but they never move around.

Brain Coral

Gulls

Birds and insects are animals that can use their legs for moving on the ground and their wings for moving in the air.

The kudu is one of the animals that walk and run on four legs.

Greater Kudu

Snakes are animals that have no legs at all. But a snake can move quite fast on rough ground.

California Kingsnake

Earthworm

An earthworm makes tunnels in the ground by eating through the dirt. It feeds on bits of plants and leaves in the dirt.

Alfalfa Butterfly

A butterfly's proboscis is like a curled tube. It uncurls its proboscis and sucks juice from flowers when it is hungry.

Animals eat

If it eats, it's an animal. And there are almost as many ways of eating as there are kinds of animals.

An earthworm eats its way through the ground. It feeds on bits of rotting plants.

A sponge takes in tiny plants and animals from the water that flows through it.

A chameleon shoots out its sticky tongue and catches insects.

A butterfly has a long, hollow strawlike mouthpart called a *proboscis* (proh BAH sihs). The butterfly keeps its proboscis rolled up. When the butterfly gets hungry, it unrolls its proboscis. It puts its proboscis into a flower and sucks up nectar.

A ground squirrel has strong teeth for cracking nuts and seeds. It carries food to its home in pockets in its cheeks.

A baleen whale takes a mouthful of seawater with tiny plants and animals in it. It lets the water run out of its mouth. Then it swallows the plants and animals.

Plants make their food from light and water and things in the ground and air. But animals must eat to live.

Sponge

Many little tunnels in a sponge's body let in seawater. In the water are tiny plants and animals the sponge eats.

The ground squirrel's cheeks are full of nuts and seeds to carry home. It cracks the shells with its strong teeth.

Golden-Mantled Ground Squirrel

Baby and Adult Mexican Bean Beetles

The baby beetle, at left, is very different from the adult. But when the baby grows up, it will look like the adult.

New living things

All living things come from other living things. Every baby animal comes from a grown-up animal like itself. A baby penguin comes from a penguin. A horse comes from a horse. A beetle comes from a beetle.

Some baby animals come right out of their mothers' bodies. Horses are born this way. So are monkeys, cats, whales, and some fish and snakes.

Some baby animals come out of eggs that come from their mothers' bodies. Penguins are born this way. So are beetles, frogs, and most fish.

Some baby animals look like their parents. Some look very different. But every baby animal grows up to be exactly the same kind of animal as its parents.

King Penguins

The baby penguin came from an egg that was laid by a mother penguin. The baby will grow to look just like her.

The foal came out of its mother's body. It looks very much like her.

Mare and Foal

Lions

As the lion cub grows up, it will learn from its mother and father many things about being a lion.

An animal grows up

Could a parrot ever roar like a lion? Could a frog learn to fly like a bird? Could a lion crack seeds as a parrot does?

None of these things could ever happen. Each baby animal grows up to live the way its parents live. It will look and act and sound like the animals of its own kind, and like no others.

A lion cub learns to walk and then run. It learns to eat meat. It growls, then it roars. It learns to hunt other animals for food.

The frog grows up and does all the things frogs do. It hops and croaks and catches insects with its sticky tongue.

The parrot learns to fly. It easily cracks nuts and seeds with its bill. It squawks with its noisy voice.

Each animal learns to live the life that all animals of its kind live. Each animal does the things it must do to stay alive. That's the way of animals.

Macaw

A parrot learns to live the way all parrots live. It flies, eats nuts and seeds, and squawks with its noisy voice.

A frog jumps and swims and croaks because its body is made to do such things. The frog can't act any other way.

Green Frog

Animals are everywhere

. . . leaping, creeping, running, and walking in forests, deserts, meadows, and snowy places.

Bat-Eared Fox

Margay Wildcat

Quarter Horse and Arabian Horse

Ribbon Seal

Kangaroo

Red-Sided Garter Snake

Animals are everywhere

. . . swimming, splashing, and floating in oceans, lakes, rivers, and ponds.

Water Beetle

Painted Turtles

Clown Sea Slug

Dolphin

Mandarin Duck

Pike

Brown Pelicans

Animals are everywhere

. . . buzzing and flapping and fluttering above the ground.

Locust

Animals are everywhere

. . . digging, squirming, and sliding below the ground.

Mole Cricket

Pocket Gopher

Mole

Bobcat

Animals are everywhere

. . . on high mountaintops . . .

Mountain Goat

Bats

Animals are everywhere

. . . in dark holes and caves.
Animals are everywhere!

Cave Cricket

Cave Salamander

Art in nature

Many beautiful creatures live on this earth. Some of them are so colorful that they look as though they were painted by a great artist.

The Wing of a Butterfly from Peru

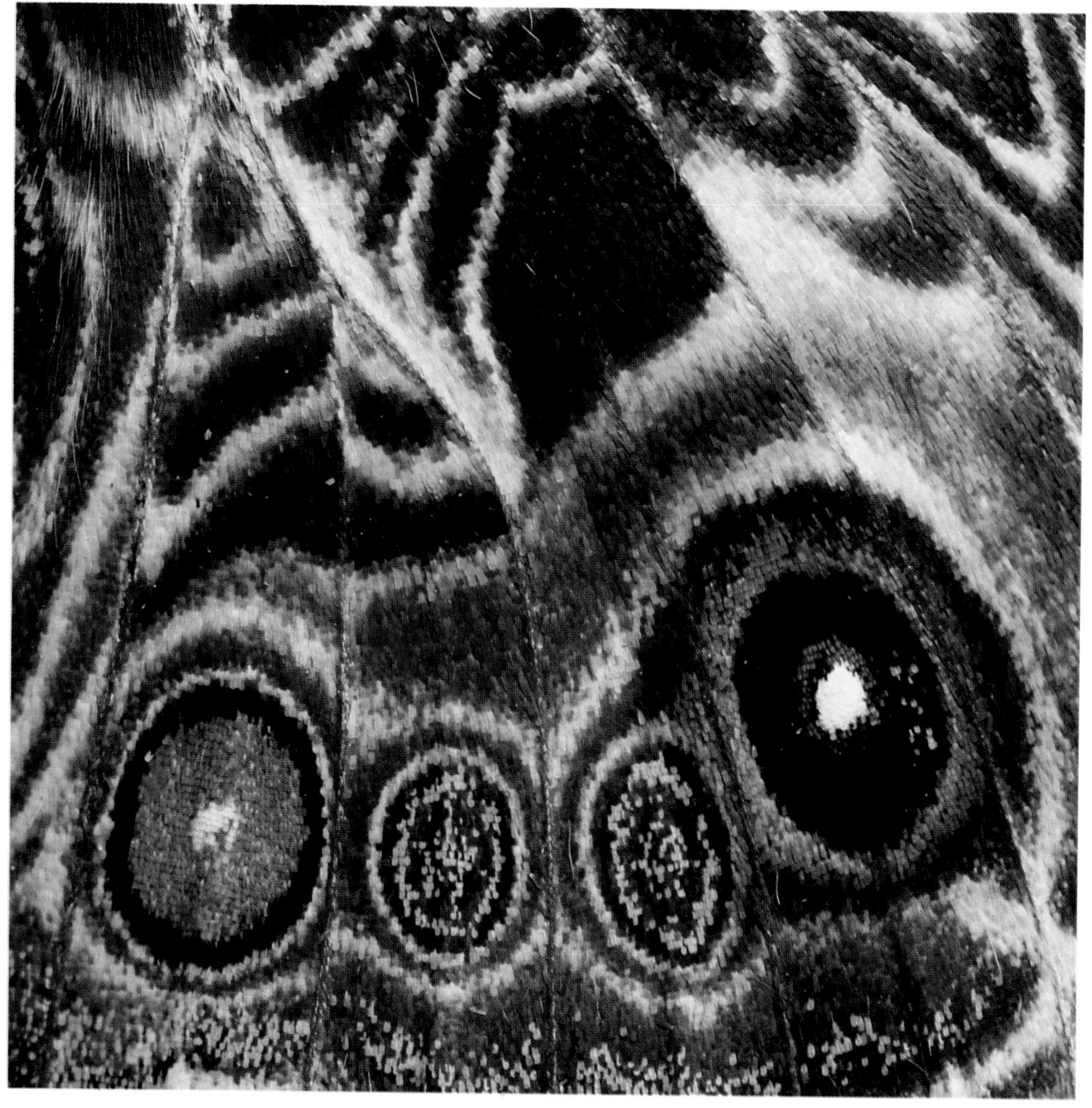

Star Tortoise from Sri Lanka

Eastern Coral Snake

Animal groups

To make it easier to study animals, scientists have arranged them into groups. All the animals in each group are alike in one or more important ways.

Mammals

If an animal drinks milk when it's a baby and has hair on its body, it belongs to the group called mammals.

Reptiles

If an animal has a scaly skin, is cold-blooded, and is always born on land, it belongs to the group called reptiles.

Amphibians

If an animal has a skeleton, is born in water and breathes with gills, but can live on land when it is grown up, it belongs to the group called amphibians.

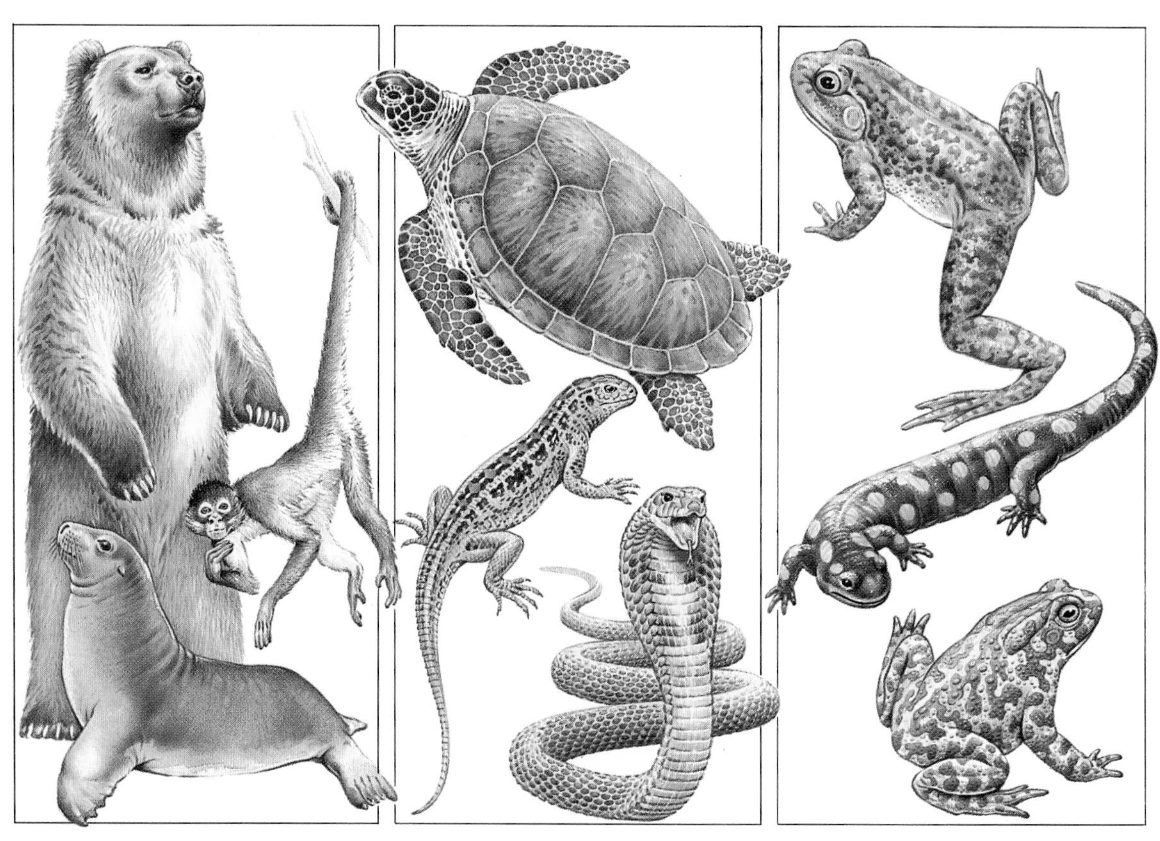

Birds

If an animal comes out of an egg with a hard shell and has feathers on its body when it grows up, it belongs to the group called birds.

Fish

If an animal lives in water and has gills and also has scales and fins on its body, it belongs to the group called fish.

Arthropods

If an animal has three or more pairs of jointed legs, a hard covering over its whole body, and no skeleton, it belongs to the group called arthropods.

Mollusks

If an animal has a soft body with no skeleton, but is normally protected by a hard shell, it belongs to the group called mollusks.

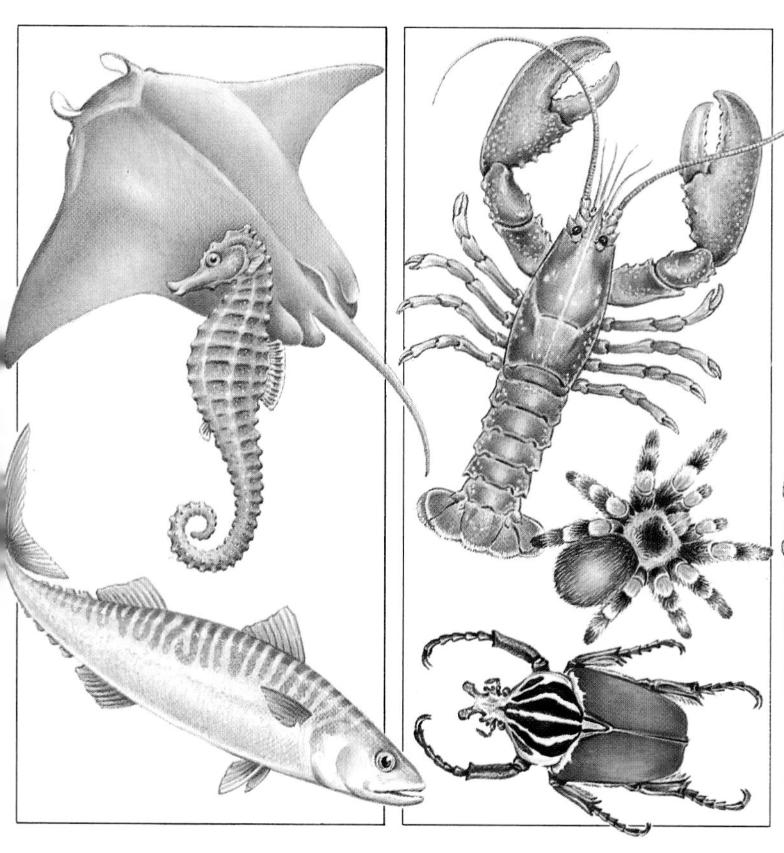

The zebra is a mammal.

It's a Mammal

Do you have a pet mammal? If you have a dog or cat you have a mammal. Hamsters and gerbils and guinea pigs are mammals, too. And so are you.

Maybe you've seen a cow feeding her calf. The calf drank milk from its mother's body. Of all the animals, only mammals do this.

Mammals are warm-blooded. The day may be freezing cold or very hot but mammals' bodies stay at just about the same temperature all the time.

Mammals have fur or hair. The fur can be short or long, straight or curly, soft or hard. There may be lots of it, or just a few thick, stiff hairs.

There are nearly one million kinds of insects and more than 21,000 kinds of fish. There are only about 4,000 kinds of mammals. But of all the animals, mammals are the ones we most often choose for our pets and helpers.

The mountain lion is a mammal.

The walrus
is a mammal.

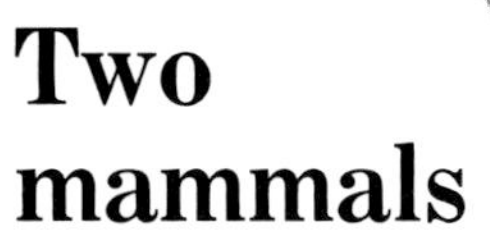

Two mammals

This is a looking page. There are lots of things to look at in this picture of a mother giraffe and her baby. What do you see?

The mother giraffe has a very long neck. You might think there would be a lot of bones in such a long neck. But the mother giraffe has no more bones in her neck than you have in yours! Her bones are just longer.

The mother giraffe's long neck and long legs make her very tall. Giraffes are the tallest of all animals.

The two giraffes have spots and squiggles on their bodies. These spots help the giraffes hide. When a giraffe goes into a bunch of trees, the spots on its body blend with the leaves. It's very, very hard to see a giraffe when it hides among trees.

The two giraffes have tails with big bunches of hair on the ends. The giraffes use their tails to brush away flies and other insects. The giraffes' bodies are covered with smooth fur. Giraffes are mammals and all mammals have some fur or hair on their bodies.

Blotched Giraffes

Mammal babies

Is a mouse like a moose? Or a dolphin like a deer? Or a bat like a cat?

These animals seem to be quite different from each other. But they're all alike in one important way. They are all mammals. And that simply means they all get the same kind of food when they are babies—milk that comes from their mothers' bodies.

Most mammal babies live inside their mothers before they are born. A baby mammal is joined to its mother by a tube. The baby gets food and oxygen from the mother's body through the tube. The baby lives and grows and when its body is ready, the baby comes out of the mother's body.

Different kinds of baby birds eat different kinds of food. So do baby fish, reptiles, insects, and amphibians.

Newborn meadow mice are not much bigger than a thimble. Their eyes are closed and they are weak and helpless.

Meadow Mice

Moose

A baby moose is born with its eyes open. It can walk in just a few hours, but it is still very weak.

But all baby mammals drink milk that comes from their mothers' bodies. Baby lions drink milk. Baby mice drink milk. Baby whales drink milk. Baby bats drink milk. No baby mammal ever gets any other kind of food until it begins to grow up.

Many kinds of mammal babies are weak and helpless for a long time. Kittens, puppies, mice, and human babies, who are mammals too, are born with weak legs. Some mammal babies are stronger. A moose calf is strong enough to follow its mother after just a few days. A pronghorn can run as fast as 25 miles (40 kilometers) an hour when it is only a day old.

Mammal babies are different in many ways, but in their kind of food, they are all alike.

Western Gray Kangaroo

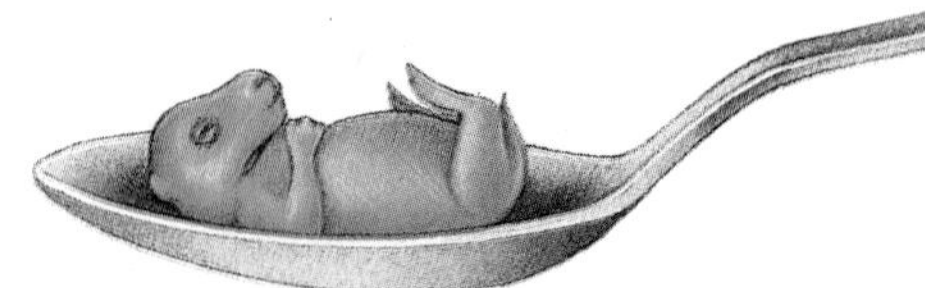

Newborn Kangaroo

A tiny newborn kangaroo could fit in a teaspoon.

Kangaroo at Eight Weeks

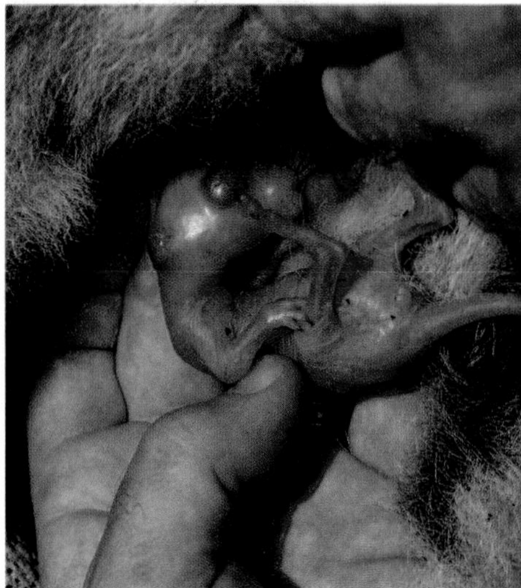

Pouch babies

A newborn kangaroo is smaller than a grown-up's thumb. A newborn koala is even smaller. And a newborn opossum is smaller still—smaller than a bee.

These are the most helpless of the mammal babies. After they are born, they spend their first months in their mothers' pouches. They don't even peek out. They just drink milk and grow.

Then for a few weeks or months they play jack-in-the-box games with their mothers. They spend part of the time out of the pouch. But they hurry back inside when they are afraid of something.

After they leave the pouches, the babies stay close to their mothers.

Opossum babies go with their mother when she looks for food. They ride on her back.

The koala baby rides piggyback. It hangs on tight as the mother koala moves through the treetops eating eucalyptus leaves. The young one stays with its mother until it is about a year old.

The kangaroo baby is called a joey. It outgrows its pouch when it is about 8 months old. Then it hops along beside its mother. It may stay with her until it is about 18 months old, or perhaps even longer.

Although these babies are tiny and weak at first, they grow into big, strong animals. The full-grown opossum is about as big as a house cat. The full-grown koala is a bit larger. The kangaroo, when it is grown, is nearly as tall as a full-grown person.

A baby koala rides piggyback wherever its mother goes.

Koala

A mother opossum takes her young for a ride.

Opossum

How mammal babies grow

The newborn meadow mouse weighs little more than a feather. Its eyes are closed and it has no fur.

The baby river otter's eyes are closed, too. But a thick fur coat covers its body.

The fawn's eyes are open. Its mother has hidden it in the bushes until it can walk. Spots on its body make it look like part of the bushes. It has no smell. A bear can walk right past and not see or smell the baby fawn.

Ten days pass. The meadow mouse now has a fur coat. Its eyes are open and it can run. It is almost grown up.

The river otter baby is still helpless. Its eyes are still closed.

The fawn can walk now. It follows its mother.

Bear and Fawn

The newborn fawn keeps still and quiet so the bear won't see it.

River Otters

Young otters love to play in the water.

A month passes. The baby otter opens its eyes. The meadow mouse is full grown. It will soon have babies of its own.

Six months pass. The fawn's spots are gone now. A bear can see it and smell it. But the fawn can run swiftly on strong legs.

The baby otter has become a champion swimmer. It loves to dive and splash and play in the water. Again and again it slides down a muddy bank into the river.

At the end of a year the fawn and the otter are nearly full grown. But the meadow mouse's life is nearly over. Each mammal baby grows its own way at its own speed.

What does it eat?

The biggest difference between mammals and all other kinds of animals is milk. Mammal mothers feed their babies milk that comes from the mothers' bodies. No other animals can do this—only mammals.

So the first food of every baby mammal is its mother's milk. Baby buffaloes and bear cubs, skunks and squirrels, whales and walruses all drink milk.

As a baby mammal grows, its jaws get strong. Its baby teeth fall out, and stronger, sharper teeth grow in their place. The little mammal learns to bite and tear and gnaw and chew. Then it needs more than milk.

Antelopes and bison need grass.

Giraffes and elephants need leaves.

Wolf pups and lion cubs need meat.

An anteater licks up termites and ants with its sticky tongue.

Giant Anteater

African Lions

Young lion cubs drink milk.

Some babies follow their mother and eat the same things she eats. But some babies need to be taught how to eat grown-up food.

A father wolf goes hunting and when he comes back, he spits out meat near his pups. The pups play with it, then they taste it. They find they like this kind of food. They become meat-eaters and never drink milk again.

Lion cubs follow their mother when she hunts. She lets them play with the animal she has killed. Once the cubs taste the meat, they learn to like it.

Every baby mammal drinks milk for a while after it is born. But as the babies grow up, they learn to eat the kind of food their mothers and fathers do.

Hippopotamus Mother and Baby

Learning days

When a baby hippopotamus starts to walk, it often tries to move away from its mother. Then she pushes it back with her big nose. Soon, the baby learns to walk near its mother, so that she can protect it.

Learning to stay near its mother is just one of many things a baby hippopotamus must learn. Baby days are learning days for hippos and all other mammals. That's when they learn the things that will help them stay alive as babies and as grown-ups.

Different kinds of mammal babies learn different ways of life. Seals will spend most of their lives in the water. Baby seals learn to swim by riding on their mothers' backs. Lion cubs, which will live by hunting, watch their mothers hunt. Baby bears learn what's good for them to eat by seeing their mother gobble berries and snatch fish out of streams.

Baby mammals learn from their mothers, although most mammal mothers don't really try to teach things to their babies. The babies watch their mothers and do the things they see her do.

A day comes when the baby mammal is nearly grown-up. It has learned how to find food and how to keep out of danger. It has learned to stay alive. Then its mother may drive it away. That's what mother moose and beaver do when their young ones are ready to live on their own.

Timber Wolves and Rabbit

Wolf cubs learn to hunt by watching an older wolf.

Where the mammals are

Mammals are everywhere. Polar bears, musk oxen, walruses, and reindeer live in some of the coldest parts of the world. Camels and kangaroo rats live in some of the warmest places. Little pikas and ground squirrels live on mountaintops. Gophers and moles live underground. Mammals make their homes in hot, tropical jungles and cool, northern forests. Whales, dolphins, and porpoises are mammals that spend their whole lives in the ocean.

Wherever there's a place to live, mammals have moved in.

Polar Bear

Some mammals live in cold, snowy places.

Dolphin

Some mammals live in the ocean.

Arabian Camel

Some mammals live in hot, dry deserts.

Rhesus Monkey

Some mammals live in hot, damp jungles.

Animal houses

Where do the animals go when winter winds blow, when snow is in the air and on the ground? Where do they hide when it's wet outside? Are little animals out when dangerous animals are about?

Some mammals need no house of any kind. Whales do not. Neither do many of

An underwater tunnel leads into the house where beavers sleep and stay warm.

Beaver Home

the hoofed animals, such as moose and musk oxen.

Some mammals look for shelter only at night or when they are having their young. Most monkeys sleep in trees. The elephant looks for a hidden spot to have her baby.

But some mammals make houses to keep out the sun or the wind or snow or other animals. The prairie dog digs a burrow with many rooms. The prairie is hot, but the burrow is cool. It is safe, too. Around the doorways are heaps of dirt. The prairie dog sits on these to look around for danger. The dirt heaps also keep out floods.

In winter, the fox is safe in its burrow deep in a sandy bank. If snow covers one, two, or three doorways, it can go out through four or five others. The muskrat's summer home of wet grass and weeds turns into a winter home of ice.

The beaver makes a house of branches and twigs. The house is often in a pond. The top of the house freezes in winter. Wind and snow and hungry animals can't get in. But the bottom of the house doesn't freeze. The beaver goes in and out to get the food it has stored at the bottom of the pond. An animal's house of whatever kind is just right for the animal that lives in it.

Squirrel Home

Some squirrels have homes in hollow trees where they store food for the winter.

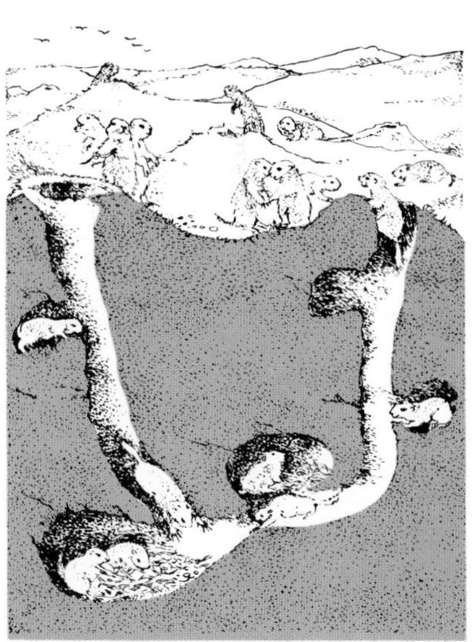

Prairie Dog Home

A prairie dog sleeps and stores food in little rooms around a tunnel.

The life of a black bear

Near winter's end, three bear cubs were born in their mother's dark, warm den. Now it is spring, and one little cub has ventured out to see the world. The other cubs will soon follow.

Mother bear settles down to feed her babies. Like all baby mammals, bear cubs drink milk.

The bear cubs find many ways to have fun. They especially like climbing a tree near the den.

While her cubs play, the mother bear takes time out for lunch. She is eating the tender, spring grasses.

A tree is a great thing to climb, and it is also a great place for a cub to take a nap.

Winter has come. The mother bear and her cubs will go back to the den for a long winter sleep.

The hummingbird is a bird.

It's a Bird

Do you know what makes a bird different from any other animal?

Not its wings. Some other animals have wings, too.

Not its bill. Some other animals have bills, too.

Not its eggs. Many other animals lay eggs.

Give up?

Feathers! All birds have feathers. And birds are the only animals that have feathers.

So if it has feathers—it's a bird!

The bald eagle is a bird.

The peacock is a bird.

The toucan
is a bird.

This bird

This is a looking page. What do you see when you look at this blue jay?

Its wings are stretched out. The feathers overlap. Because they overlap, the feathers catch and hold the air. They help the bird fly.

The bird's tail feathers overlap, too. They help the bird steer itself when it flies, and they help the bird land.

The bird has claws on its feet. The claws help the bird perch on the birch log.

If you could touch this bird, you would find that it has two kinds of feathers. The feathers you see are stiff. Under these, next to the bird's skin, is a layer of soft feathers called ***down***. Down helps keep the bird warm. Some birds line their nests with down.

Blue Jay

Ostriches

The baby ostrich on the left has been out of its egg for several minutes. Its feathers are beginning to dry. The other baby ostrich is just breaking out of its egg. In a moment, it will push itself all the way out.

Coming out of the egg

Inside its egg the tiny baby bird lies curled up in a ball. Its head is bigger than its body. Its eyes are closed. All of the food it will need is inside the egg.

The baby bird grows until it fills the inside of the egg. Then it is ready to hatch.

Many kinds of baby birds have a tiny tooth near the tip of the bill. A baby bird uses this tooth to help break the eggshell. A few days after the bird hatches, or leaves the egg, the tooth will either disappear or fall off.

When the baby is ready to hatch, it begins to move inside the egg. The eggshell cracks. The baby bird scrapes its tooth against the crack and the crack grows bigger. Pieces of the shell fall off.

After a while the baby bird has made a big hole in the shell. The baby bird wiggles through the hole. A new life has come into the world.

Baby birds

Some baby robins lie close together in a nest. Their eyes are closed. They have no feathers. They can't stand on their tiny, weak legs.

With a flutter of wings the mother robin lands on the nest. In her bill is a wiggling worm. At once, each baby's mouth opens wide. "Me! Me! Give it to me!" each open mouth seems to be saying.

The mother pushes the worm into a mouth and flies away. She'll be back soon with another worm or insect. Then another baby bird will have its turn to eat.

On a pile of grass near a river are some baby ducks. They are different from the robins. The little ducks have fuzzy feathers. Their bright eyes are wide open. And when their mother quacks, they follow her out of the nest. All in a row they waddle to the river for a swim.

Some kinds of birds, such as robins, blue jays, and nuthatches, are helpless for several weeks after they hatch. But other kinds of birds, such as flamingos, ducks, chickens, and geese, can see and walk and care for themselves soon after they hatch.

Robins

Baby robins are weak and helpless. Their parents have to feed them.

A baby flamingo leaves its nest about five days after it hatches.

Flamingos

Birds that fly and birds that don't

A baby swift is getting ready to fly. Ever since it hatched, its feathers have been getting longer. Its wings have been growing stronger. Now, the little bird is ready.

It hops to the edge of the nest. Even though it has never flown, the swift knows just what to do. It spreads its wings and pushes itself off the nest with its legs. Air pushes up on the swift's wings and holds the little bird up. The swift flaps its wings. Feathers on the ends of the wings spread out and twist. This pulls air under each wing and pulls the baby swift forward.

Many birds can fly well the very first time they try. Some birds, such as sparrows, need a little practice. They flutter weakly out of the nest. Then they hop about on the ground, flapping their wings for a few days before they can really fly.

Swifts and sparrows and all the other birds you see every day can fly. So it may surprise you to learn that there are some birds that *can't* fly.

Ostriches can't fly. Their wings are just too small to lift their big bodies into the air.

Penguins can't fly. Their wings are like a seal's flippers. Penguins use their wings for swimming. Penguins can swim as well as fish can.

And the birds called kiwis can't fly. Their wings are very tiny and can hardly be seen.

Some of the flying birds are the fastest of all animals. The fastest bird is the duck hawk. In a dive, it can reach a speed of 200 miles (320 kilometers) an hour!

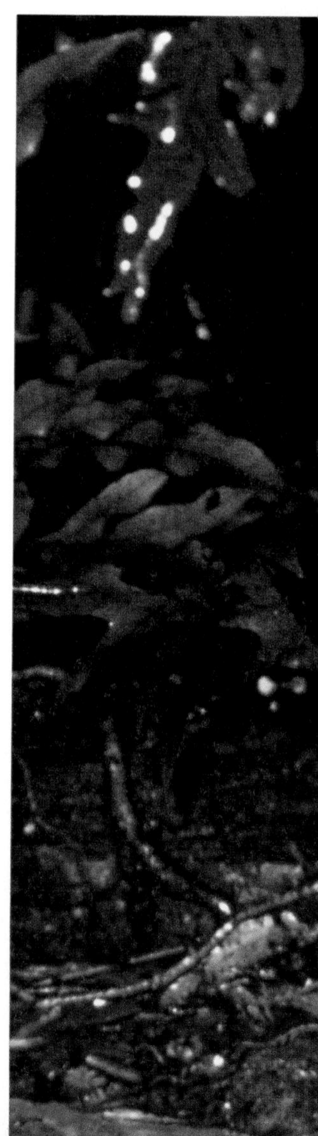

Chimney Swift

Most birds can fly.

This bird can't fly.

Kiwi

Shovels, spears, and nutcrackers

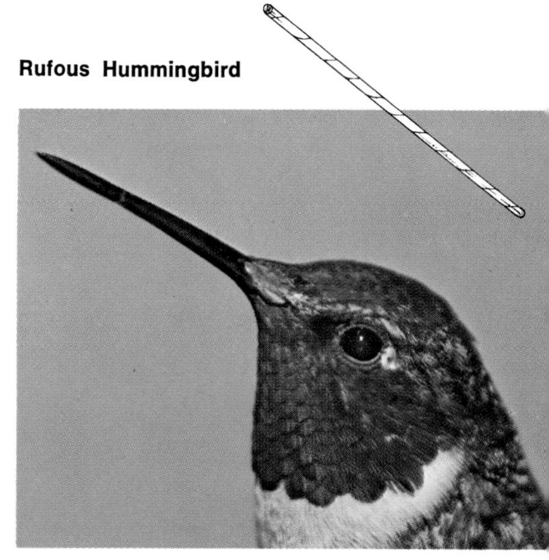
Rufous Hummingbird

A roseate spoonbill wades by the seashore with its head underwater. Its bill is like a shovel. It swings its head from side to side and shovels tiny fish and other food from the mud and water.

A heron's bill is like a spear. It is long and pointed. A heron may stick its sharp bill into fish, lift them out of the water, and swallow them.

A parrot's bill is like a nutcracker. A parrot can easily crack open nuts and seeds with its big, strong bill.

Robins and sparrows eat things they find on the ground. Robins' and sparrows' bills are like tweezers. Their bills make it easy for them to pick up things.

Pileated Woodpecker

A woodpecker's bill is like a chisel. A woodpecker eats insects that live under the bark of trees. The woodpecker pounds its bill against a tree and the sharp, pointed bill makes a hole in the bark. Then the woodpecker can get at the insects.

A hummingbird's bill is long and narrow, like a straw. The hummingbird sticks its bill deep into a flower and uses its long tongue to sip up nectar.

Most birds' bills are special tools. They are shaped to help the bird get the kind of food it eats.

Louisiana Heron

Savannah Sparrow

Blue Parrot

Roseate Spoonbill

Homes for baby birds

Nests are the homes that birds make for their babies. The mother birds lay their eggs in the nests. After the baby birds hatch, they are cared for in the nests until they grow up. Then all the birds leave the nests.

Different kinds of birds build different kinds of nests. Many birds make nests in trees. Robins make bowl-shaped nests in trees. They use anything they can find, such as grass, twigs, leaves, and string. They line the inside of their nests with mud. Then they cover the mud with grass.

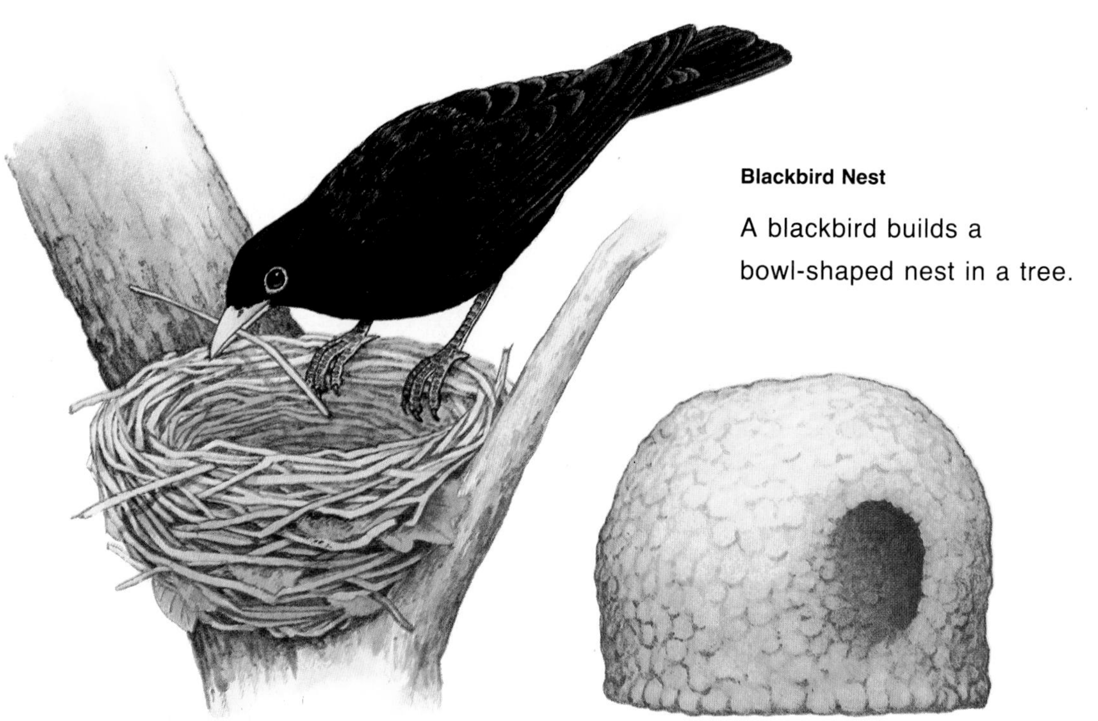

Blackbird Nest

A blackbird builds a bowl-shaped nest in a tree.

Ovenbird Nest

The ovenbird's dome-shaped nest has two rooms.

Weaverbird Nest

A weaverbird uses its bill to weave a hanging nest of grass and sticks.

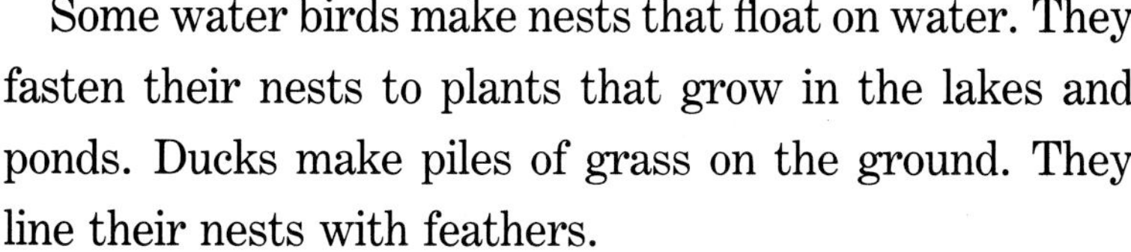

Oriole Nest

An oriole builds a nest that looks like a pouch hanging from a tree limb.

Some water birds make nests that float on water. They fasten their nests to plants that grow in the lakes and ponds. Ducks make piles of grass on the ground. They line their nests with feathers.

Ovenbirds make dome-shaped nests that look somewhat like old-fashioned ovens. The ovenbird got its name from the kind of nest it builds.

Some birds don't build their own nests. Some of them just lay their eggs in hollow places in tree trunks. Others, such as cowbirds and European cuckoos, lay their eggs in the nests of other birds.

The life of a Canada goose

In early spring a pair of Canada geese pick each other as mates. The female, at left, will soon lay eggs.

The female makes a nest of grass and feathers. She nestles on her eggs, warming them.

Look out! An animal is nearby. The goose beats her wings, hisses, and honks. This frightens the animal away.

Nearly a month passes. Then the wet, weak little goslings push out of their eggs into the world.

Turn the page to see the rest of this picture story.

The life of a Canada goose

The goslings can walk almost at once. After a day, they leave the nest to look around.

Goslings swim and dive without being taught. Their parents protect them as they swim.

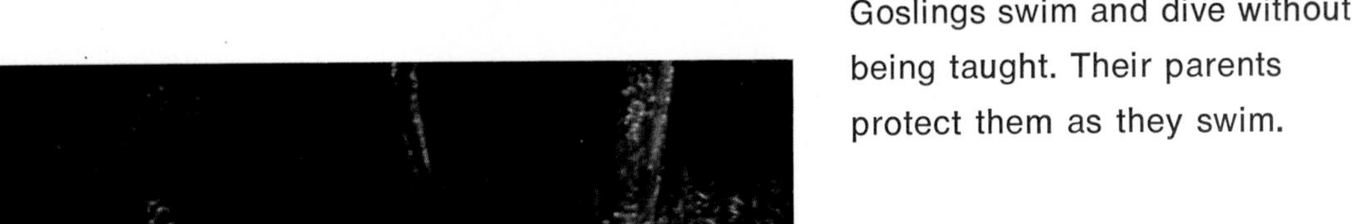

The 2-week-old goslings waddle about from place to place, learning about life.

Now, summer is nearly over.
The goslings are 2 months old—
nearly old enough to fly.

In the fall, families of geese make ready to fly south. In two or more years, the young geese will be ready to have families of their own.

A sea horse is a fish.

It's a Fish

Sometimes it's hard to tell what's a fish and what isn't. A sea horse doesn't look like a fish, but it is. And a dolphin looks like a fish, but it isn't!

How can you tell if an animal is a fish? Well, nearly all fish have scales. Scales are little round or diamond-shaped pieces of thin bony stuff. They fit together over the fish's whole body.

And nearly all fish have fins. A fish usually has a fin on its back, a fin on its belly, a broad fin for a tail, and two fins on each side.

And all fish have gills. Gills are slits in a fish's head, behind its mouth. Fish breathe with gills.

Scales, fins, and gills—if it has all these things, it's a fish!

A perch is a fish.

An eel is a fish.

This is a triggerfish.

This fish

This is a looking page. What does the picture tell you about the fish?

This fish has shiny scales. Scales are like small, thin pieces of fingernail that cover a fish's body.

This fish has big, staring eyes. Its eyes are always open because it has no eyelids.

This fish has fins on its back and underside. The fish steers itself with its fins as it swims. It swims by wiggling its broad tail.

On the fish's head, just above the front fins, are the fish's gills. Every fish has gills.

Gills are what a fish breathes with. They are openings filled with thin pieces of skin like the pages of a book. Water goes into the openings and through the "pages." They take the oxygen out of the water and put the oxygen into the fish's blood. Like all animals, a fish must have oxygen to live.

Brown Trout

Champion egg layers

Some fish don't lay eggs. Some fish lay a few eggs. Some fish lay thousands of eggs, and some fish lay millions of eggs.

A mother herring may lay more than forty thousand eggs at a time. The eggs drop down in the water and stick to sand, rocks, or plants. A mother sardine may lay more than eighty thousand eggs. Her eggs float in the water.

The champion egg layer is the ocean sunfish, which may lay as many as 300 million eggs.

With millions of fish laying millions of eggs, you might think the oceans, lakes, and rivers would be filled with baby fish. But most fish eggs never hatch. Fish eggs have no shells to protect them. They are round and soft like bits of jelly. Many eggs wash ashore and dry up. Many are gobbled up by other fish. Only a few eggs out of every million ever become adult fish.

Jewel Cichlids

This fish lays hundreds of eggs
that stick to rocks and sand.
Some fish lay millions of eggs
that float in the water.

Finny fathers

In the world of fish, it is often the father that does most of the baby-sitting.

A father smallmouth black bass starts to take care of his babies even before they're hatched. He makes a wide, saucer-shaped hole in the sand. The mother bass lays her eggs in the hole. The eggs are sticky. They stick to the sand and do not float away.

After the mother lays the eggs, the father pushes her away. He wants to guard the eggs all by himself. He swims back and forth over the nest. He fans the eggs

When the eggs hatch, baby sea horses shoot out of their father's pouch.

Sea horse

A father sea horse keeps the mother's eggs in a pouch on his stomach.

Stickleback

This fish is guarding eggs in a nest.

with his tail. This keeps the water around the eggs fresh and helps them hatch.

When the babies hatch they cannot swim well at first. The father watches over them. He fights anything that comes near. When the babies can swim, the father swims with them and guards them while they find food.

Many other father fish make nests and guard their babies as a father smallmouth black bass does. But a father sea catfish protects his babies in a different way. He keeps the eggs in his mouth until they hatch. When they hatch, he holds the babies in his mouth until they're big enough to take care of themselves. Then he spits them out into the water and away they swim.

Fish food

Nearly everything that lives in the water is food for a hungry fish.

In the ocean, most fish eat only other fish. Ocean cod, hake, tarpon, and tuna dine on smaller herrings, sardines, and anchovies. And the big fish are themselves gulped down by sharks. Sharks will eat any animal, dead or alive.

In rivers and lakes, fish eat fish, too. But some of them add other tasty things to their fish diet. Trout jump out of the water to snap at flying insects. Sturgeons dine on snails, crayfish, and insects. Big, hungry bass, pike, and bowfins gobble up frogs, baby ducks, and even baby muskrats.

Some kinds of fish eat only plants. Carp and suckermouth catfish swim along at the bottom of rivers and ponds. With tiny teeth they chew up bits of plants that grow in the mud.

A few kinds of fish eat both plants and animals. Parrot fish eat seaweed and tiny worms that live in coral. The ocean sunfish eats tiny shrimps, baby fish, jellyfish, and tiny plants called algae.

A Pumpkinseed Sunfish Eating a Worm

Freshwater Fish

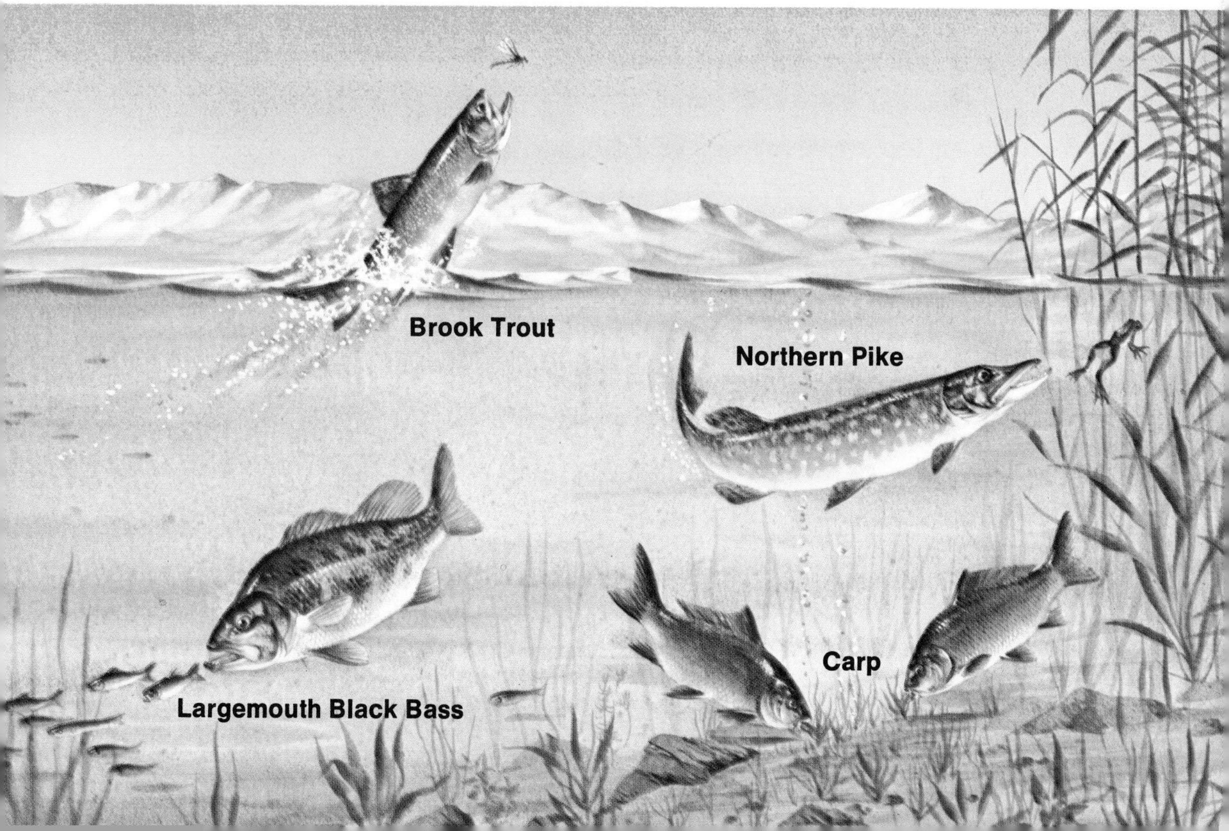

Brook Trout

Northern Pike

Largemouth Black Bass

Carp

Mudskippers

Archerfish

Which is the strangest fish?

Cowfish

There are thousands of kinds of fishes. If you tried to choose the strangest fish in the world, you'd have a hard time.

The mudskipper has a head like a frog and a body like a fish. It often crawls onto land. It can jump up and catch flying insects in its mouth.

An archerfish can shoot its food. The archerfish swims at the top of the water. A beetle comes buzzing past. The fish shoots a stream of water from its mouth. The water hits the beetle and it falls down. The archerfish gobbles it up.

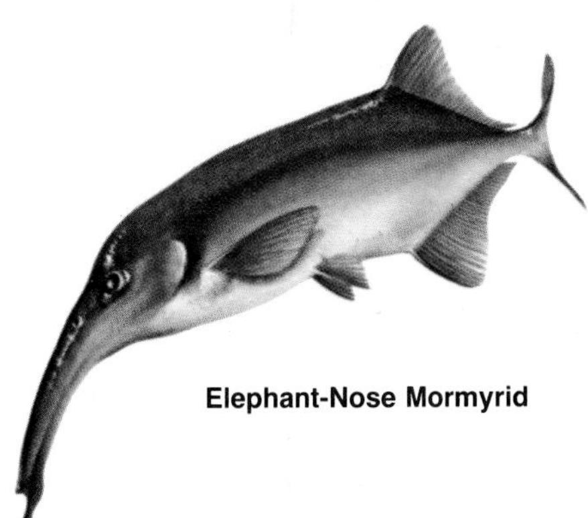

Elephant-Nose Mormyrid

A fish called a cowfish has points on its head that look like horns.

The elephant-nose mormyrid has a long nose that looks like an elephant's trunk.

A puffer fish can fill itself with air. It looks like a round balloon with eyes and a mouth.

Leafy sea dragons look like pieces of seaweed. A flounder has both eyes on one side of its body. You can see the insides of a glass catfish.

These are just a few of the strange fish that live in the world. See what a hard time you'd have trying to choose the strangest?

Southern Puffer

Grunts, croaks, snores, and roars

The ocean is a noisy place! It's full of grunts, croaks, squeaks, snores, clicks, and roars. Many of these sounds are made by fish.

Some fish are named after the sounds they make. One kind of fish rubs its teeth together to make a grunting noise. So the fish is called a grunt.

Another kind of fish makes a croaking noise that sounds like *boop-boop-boop-boop*. That fish is called a croaker. And can you guess what kind of noise is made by the fish called a snorer?

Pollack, haddock, toadfishes, and many other fish also make grunting noises. They grunt by snapping some of their muscles against a piece of skin inside their bodies. Sea horses make a clicking noise by hitting a piece of bone on their heads against a piece of bone on their backs.

Sharks sometimes make a roaring noise. But they aren't really roaring—they're burping! Many sharks swallow air to keep their bodies up near the top of the water. When they want to go deeper they have to burp up the air. The burp sounds like a roar.

Noises such as the shark's roar have no meaning. But some fish noises seem to mean something. Many of them seem to be made by male fish calling to female fish. Some of them are made by fish getting ready to fight. Scientists study fish noises to see if all these grunts, croaks, and clicks mean anything.

Splendid Toadfish

The toadfish makes a noise by snapping one of its muscles against a piece of skin.

White Grunts

The grunt gets its name from the grunting noise it makes by rubbing its teeth together.

A gila monster is a reptile.

It's a Reptile

Suppose you found some hard-shelled eggs lying on the ground. And suppose that some little scaly skinned creatures hatched out of them. What *kind* of animal would they be?

They could only be reptiles.

Fish have a scaly skin—but fish eggs do not have hard shells. And most fish lay their eggs in water, not on land.

Bird eggs have hard shells, and are always laid on land—but birds don't have a scaly skin.

Only reptiles have a scaly skin and lay hard-shelled eggs on land. That's one way to tell an animal *is* a reptile.

Alligators, crocodiles, lizards, snakes, turtles and tuataras are reptiles.

A crocodile is a reptile.

A green sea turtle is a reptile.

This reptile is a python.

This reptile

This is a looking page. Look at this turtle.

The turtle's head looks as if an artist had painted stripes and spots on it. That's why this kind of turtle is called a painted turtle.

The turtle's shell looks hard and shiny and bumpy. When the turtle fears danger it pulls its head, legs, and tail into the shell. The shell is too hard for most animals to bite through. So when the turtle hides in its shell it is usually safe.

Look at the turtle's toes. On each toe there is a sharp little claw. The turtle's feet are webbed. Do you think this helps the turtle swim better?

The turtle looks as if it is getting ready to go into the water. It doesn't look as if it could swim well because of its hard, heavy shell. But this kind of turtle is a good swimmer.

Painted Turtle

Meet the reptiles

You can always tell a turtle by its shell. A box turtle has a high, round shell that it can close up like a box. A map turtle has a wide, flat shell with bumpy edges. A soft-shelled turtle's shell looks like a green pancake. Most turtles can pull their heads, legs, and tails into their shells at the first sign of danger.

You can always tell a snake by its shape. Whether it's a little ringneck snake 15 inches (38 centimeters) long, or a big 30-foot (9-meter) anaconda, every snake is long, round, and legless.

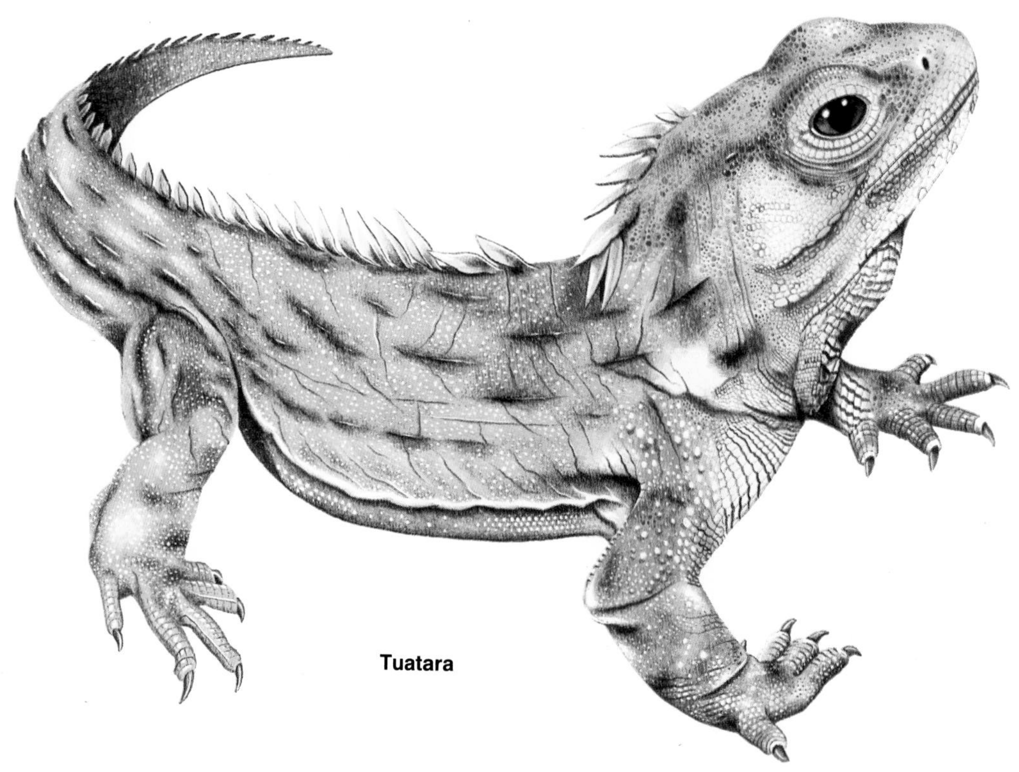

Tuatara

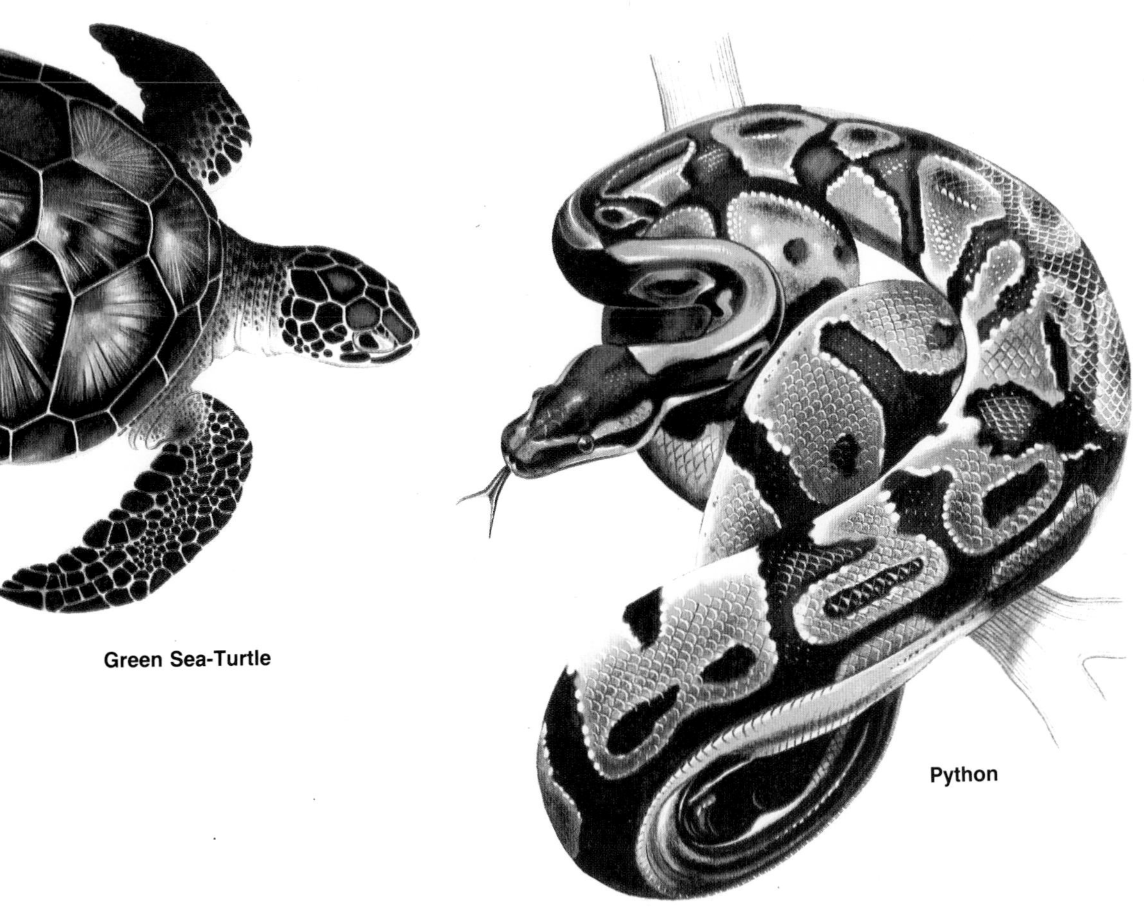

Green Sea-Turtle

Python

Sometimes it's hard to tell what's a lizard and what isn't. Some lizards look like snakes and some look like worms and some lizards look like baby alligators. But there's one way to tell geckos, skinks, and some other lizards. If an animal grabs one of these lizards by the tail—the tail comes off and the lizard runs away. It doesn't hurt these lizards to lose their tails. And they soon grow new ones.

Alligators and crocodiles, the biggest reptile, look very much alike. But an alligator has fatter, shorter jaws, and it is smaller.

Scaly babies and mothers

A large American alligator crawls into some thorny bushes. She pulls up bushes with her mouth. She stamps her feet. Soon, she has made a wide, clear place. She makes a pile of mud and plants. She scoops a hole in the top of the pile and lays as many as fifty eggs in the hole. Then she covers the eggs with mouthfuls of mud and plants.

For two months the mother alligator stays by her nest. One day she hears little grunting noises. She tears the nest open with her teeth. Tiny baby alligators blink at the sudden bright sunshine.

Alligators take care of their eggs until they hatch. But most reptile mothers just lay their eggs and leave. Their babies never see them.

Mother turtles dig holes in mud or sand. They lay their eggs in the holes. Then they cover up the eggs and go away. The warm sun hatches the eggs. The baby turtles dig their way out of the nest and crawl to the water.

Most mother snakes just lay their eggs and crawl away, too. But a few kinds of snakes wrap themselves around their eggs until they hatch. When the eggs hatch, the mothers leave.

A mother alligator puts her eggs inside a nest of mud and grass. When the eggs hatch, the mother tears the nest open.

American Alligators

New skins for old

A shiny garter snake wiggles through the grass. Its wrinkled old skin hangs from the tip of its tail. The snake comes to some rocks. It slides between them. The old skin catches on one of the rocks. With a twist of its tail, the snake crawls on. The old skin stays behind.

Every few months a snake grows too big for its skin. Each time, it gets rid of its old skin by crawling right out of it.

When the old skin is ready to come off, it dries up and becomes loose. Then the snake rubs its mouth against

When a snake crawls out of its old skin, its new skin is very shiny.

Pilot Black Snake

Tokay Gecko

This lizard has pulled off all but a few pieces of its old skin.

something rough. The skin around its lips splits and opens up. This doesn't hurt the snake.

The snake starts to crawl. As it crawls, its old skin turns inside out and slides down the snake's body. At last, the old skin just hangs from the snake's tail. The snake crawls between some rocks or some branches. Off comes the old skin. Away crawls the snake in a shiny new skin that grew beneath the old one.

Lizards take off their old skins, too. But because of their legs, they can't get the skins off in one piece as a snake can. The lizards tear off their old skins in pieces. And some lizards eat the pieces.

Suppers for snakes

Snakes eat only live food. Most snakes eat rats, birds, lizards, and rabbits. Small snakes eat mice, worms, frogs, snails, and insects. Snakes called hook-nosed snakes eat mostly spiders. African egg-eating snakes eat only birds' eggs.

But guess what the favorite food of some snakes is? It's other snakes! Black racer snakes eat more snakes than any other kind of food. King snakes and cobras eat lots of other snakes, too.

African Egg-Eating Snake

Snakes can swallow things that are bigger than their heads. This snake is going to swallow a whole chicken egg.

The snake's jaws come apart and its skin stretches. The water in its mouth helps the egg slide easily.

Snakes don't chew their food. They swallow it whole. Snakes can open their mouths very wide. Their heads and bodies stretch to let in big things.

Egg-eating snakes can swallow eggs that are bigger than their heads.

Little garter snakes can swallow whole frogs.

And big pythons can swallow whole hogs, small deer, or goats, hoofs and all!

A bone in the snake's throat will crack the shell. Then the snake will spit out the pieces.

Moving without legs

Snakes have no legs at all, but they move quite well without them. A snake can go zig-zagging over the ground just about as fast as you can walk.

Most snakes leave a wiggly trail when they crawl. They do this because they curve their bodies into one S shape after another. The top, middle, and bottom parts of the S push against the ground. This makes the snake slide forward.

The sidewinder snake moves sideways. It folds itself up like a spring. Then it stretches its head out as far as it can and lays it on the ground. It pushes hard against

Green Python

(above) A green python uses its belly scales to help it move forward or climb. (right) A sidewinder crawls by jumping along the ground sideways.

the ground and pulls the rest of its body alongside its head. Each time the sidewinder pulls itself sideways, its body leaves the ground a little way. So the sidewinder is really hopping along instead of crawling along! Instead of leaving a wiggly trail, it leaves a trail like a row of I's.

Some snakes crawl on the large, flat scales of their undersides. Pythons and rattlers and boas do this. They push the scales forward. The scales dig into the ground. The snake then pulls its body up to the scales. This makes it slide forward in a straight line.

It seems as if it would be hard to move without legs. But snakes do it well.

Sidewinder Rattlesnake

Playing hide and seek with the sun

It is night in a desert. A small lizard lies covered with sand. Only its head sticks out. It is using the sand like a blanket to keep its body warm during the cool night.

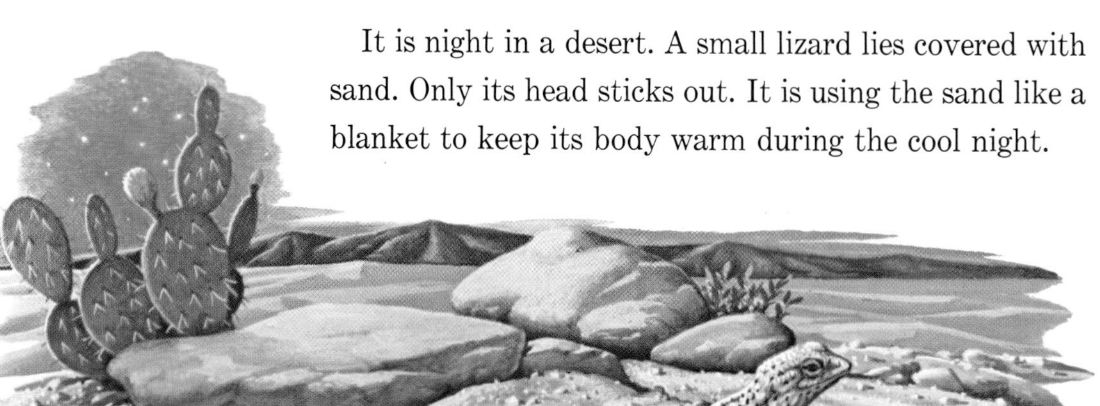

When the sun comes up, the lizard crawls out of the sand. It moves very slowly because it is cold. It lies on a rock for a long time, letting the sun warm it.

When its body is warm enough, the lizard dashes off to look for food.

Many times during the day, the lizard's body grows too hot in the bright sunshine. Then it crawls into the shade of a rock until its body cools off a little.

Fringed-Toed Iguanid

Lizards and all other reptiles are cold-blooded. Their bodies get just as hot or cold as the air or water around them. If their bodies get cold, reptiles can't move well. And if their bodies get too hot, reptiles die. So reptiles must help their bodies by playing hide and seek with the sun. If they are cold, they lie in warm sunshine. If they are hot, they hurry into shade. Alligators, crocodiles, and most turtles go into cool water when they are hot.

A reptile that lives where winters are cold moves more and more slowly as cold weather comes. The reptile curls up in the warmest hole it can find. Its body grows cold and stiff. It cannot move at all. Only when warm weather returns can the reptile move and start its life again.

The European green toad is an amphibian.

It's an Amphibian

Did you ever see a big, fat frog? A frog is one of the animals that lives in water when it is a baby and on land when it grows up. We call these animals amphibians.

Amphibians lay eggs that are soft and have no shells. The eggs dry up easily, so amphibians must lay them in water or wet places. Most baby amphibians are born in water. They look like baby fish and breathe with gills as a fish does.

When most amphibians grow up their gills disappear. Then the amphibians come on land to live. They breathe with lungs as birds, dogs, and people do.

The word *amphibian* means *two lives.* That's a good name for animals that live one kind of life in water and another kind of life on land.

The spotted salamander is an amphibian.

The red-eyed tree frog
is an amphibian.

This amphibian

This is a looking page. It can show you many things about this frog, if you look carefully.

See the frog's big, round eyes? They are on the very top of its head. The frog can peek out of the water without having to stick its whole head above water. Do you think this helps the frog stay safer?

The frog's back legs look big and strong, don't they? Big, strong back legs are what make the frog such a wonderful jumper. And the frog does all its swimming with its back legs.

The feet on the frog's back legs are like big flippers. They help the frog swim.

The frog's front legs are smaller than its back legs. The frog rests its front feet on the ground when it sits. Sometimes it uses its front feet like hands, to push insects and other food into its mouth.

Look at the frog's skin. If you could touch it, do you think it would feel bumpy or smooth?

Water Frog

Amphibians all

Frogs and toads look much alike. But toads are fatter than frogs and have shorter back legs. A toad's skin is rough and damp. A frog's skin is smooth and wet. Most toads have warts on their skin. But you won't catch warts if you touch a toad.

Frogs and toads have no tails. The amphibians called salamanders and newts all have tails. There are many kinds of newts and salamanders. Pygmy salamanders, which live in the United States, are no longer than one of your fingers. Giant salamanders, which live in Japan, are longer than you are tall.

The strangest of all the amphibians are the caecilians. Caecilians live in tropical lands. They look like big, fat worms. Sometimes they are as big around as a man's thumb and as long as his leg.

Caecilian

Newts

Mud Puppy (Salamander)

Green Frog and American Toad

Red Salamander

Amphibians go hunting

Most kinds of amphibians hide and sleep during the day. At night they come creeping and hopping out to hunt for food.

Frogs and toads seem to be always hungry. And, in a way, they're a lot like lions and tigers because they hunt for live things to eat. Frogs and toads eat insects, worms, and even smaller frogs or toads. Big bullfrogs will even eat small turtles, snakes, mice, and birds.

Frogs and toads will eat only things that move. An

The earthworm this toad caught was longer than the toad. But the toad will swallow it all down.

American Toad

Common Frog

The frog has caught a bush cricket. It will use its front feet to push the cricket down into its mouth.

insect or worm might be safe right in front of a frog or toad if it didn't move. But if it makes even the tiniest wiggle, the frog or toad will see it and gulp it down.

Many kinds of frogs and toads have long, sticky tongues that they use for catching food. If an insect comes near them, the frog or toad will slowly move closer —and closer. Then—*snap!* The tongue shoots out and pulls the insect into the amphibian's mouth.

Frogs and toads are skillful hunters. A scientist once watched a small toad catch 52 mosquitoes—in less than a minute!

Hiding from winter

Amphibians are cold-blooded. Their bodies are just about as warm or as cold as the air or water around them. So when winter comes, and the days get colder, an amphibian's body gets colder, too.

The amphibians try to get warm. Frogs and toads creep into deep holes that they find or dig. Many kinds of newts and salamanders crawl beneath logs, stones, or piles of leaves. Some salamanders and frogs dig into the bottom of the pond or river in which they live.

The weather turns colder. The frogs, toads, and salamanders huddle in their hiding places. Their bodies grow

Spotted Salamander in Winter

cold. They cannot move. Their breathing slows down and their hearts nearly stop beating. They must stay this way all through the cold days and nights of winter. And if their hiding places are not deep enough or warm enough, their bodies will grow so cold that they will die.

When spring comes along to warm up the world again, the amphibians begin to warm up, too. A few at a time they creep out of their hiding places. Then you begin to hear the *peep-peep* of the tree frogs and the *chuggerum* of the bullfrogs as the amphibians start their lives once more.

Spotted Salamander in Spring

The life of a grass frog

In early spring, the mother grass frog lays a thousand or more eggs in a lake or pond. Five days later, tiny wiggly tadpoles come out of the eggs.

The tadpoles swim about, nibbling at plants. They breathe with gills, like fish. But lungs for breathing air are growing in their bodies.

After two months, the tadpoles grow little legs. A few weeks later they grow arms. Many tadpoles are eaten by fish and water insects.

By summer's end, the frogs are full grown. During winter they will hibernate at the bottom of the pond. In the spring they will become fathers and mothers of new little tadpoles.

After three months, the tadpoles can leave the water and breathe air with their lungs. They are now young frogs. Their short, tadpole tails will shrink away and vanish.

A tussock moth caterpillar
is an arthropod.

Many-Legged Creatures

Any sunny, summer day, in almost any back yard, empty lot, or lawn, you can see dozens of wild animals!

You're sure to see the eight-legged creature that catches other animals in a trap. It's a spider! And you may get to see the wonderful six-legged jumping animal that has its ears on its sides. It's a grasshopper! And if you find a ring of clay around a hole, it may be the front door of the ten-legged tunnel builder called a crayfish!

The world is full of these many-legged creatures. They are called arthropods. They live everywhere—jungles, deserts, oceans, caves, mountaintops, and in your back yard, where you can watch them creep, crawl, hop, dash, fly, hunt, fight, and eat, all summer long.

A ladybug
is an arthropod.

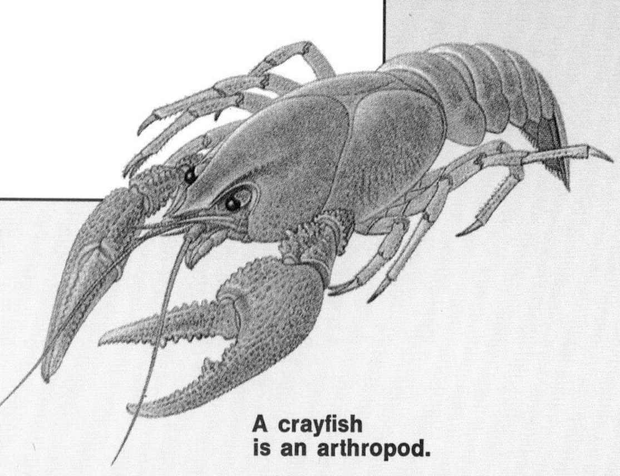

A crayfish
is an arthropod.

A grasshopper
is an arthropod.

Six legs

Did a fly ever land on your arm and tickle you? It was tickling with its six legs as it walked on your skin.

A fly is one of the six-legged animals we call insects. Flies, ants, bees, grasshoppers, beetles, crickets, and butterflies are all insects. They all have six legs.

All insects also have two wiggly feelers on their heads. And most kinds of insects have wings. Some, such as flies, have two wings. Some, such as dragonflies and beetles, have four wings.

All insects have six legs and two feelers. Most insects have wings. And all insects' bodies are divided into three parts—head, chest, and stomach.

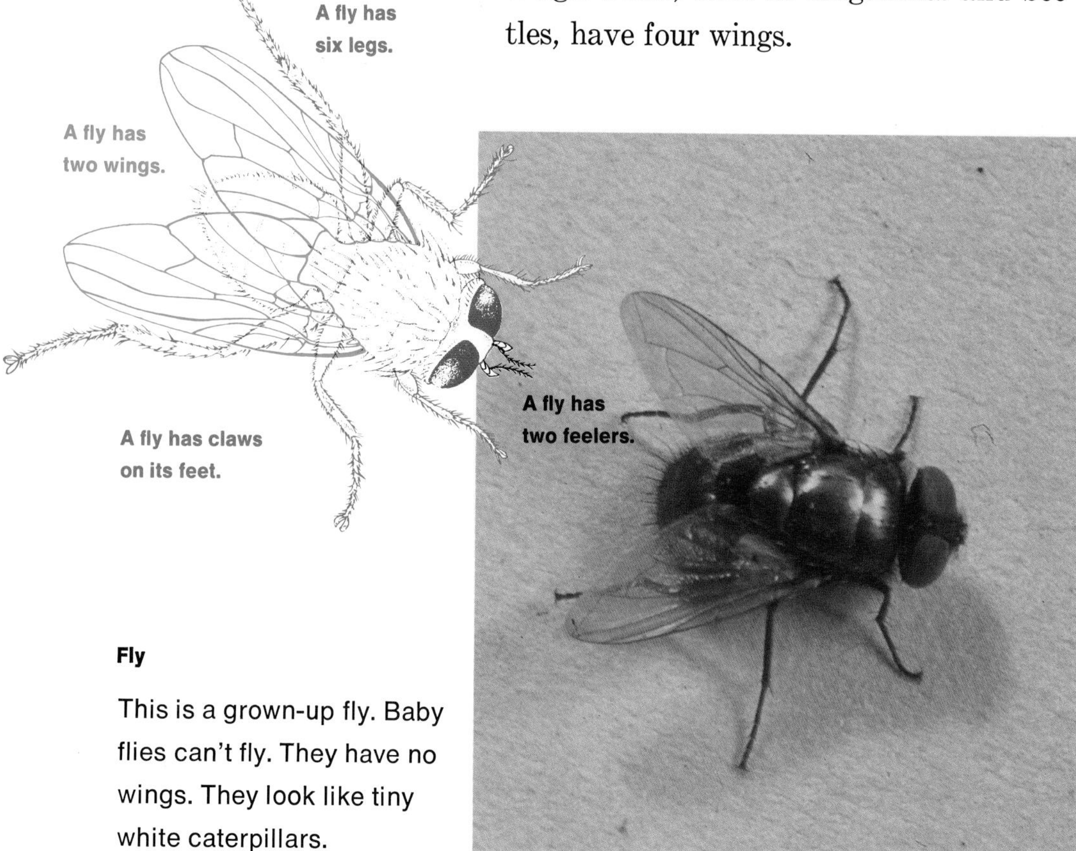

Fly

This is a grown-up fly. Baby flies can't fly. They have no wings. They look like tiny white caterpillars.

Insects are not at all like people. If you want to taste something, you put your tongue on it. But if a fly wants to taste something it walks on it. A fly tastes with its feet. When you want to smell something, you put your nose near it. But a fly has no nose. It smells things with the two feelers on its head. The fly can smell things better with its feelers than you can with your nose.

Insects don't see as we do either. Most insects have eyes that are really hundreds of tiny eyes. Each tiny eye sees a piece of what the insect is looking at. This must make the insect see everything as though it were looking through a screen.

No matter where you live, some of these little six-legged animals are sure to be near you. There are nearly a million kinds of insects—and there are billions of each kind!

Long-Horned Milkweed Beetle

All insects have feelers. This beetle's feelers are quite long. Some insects have shorter ones.

Dragonfly

Some insects, such as this dragonfly, have four wings. Some insects have two wings.

Eight legs

Many people don't like spiders. But spiders help us. They eat many insects that are harmful to people.

Some spiders trap insects in webs made of silk. The silk comes out of tiny holes in the spider's body. The silk is a liquid that becomes a thin, strong thread when air touches it.

Different kinds of spiders make different kinds of webs. Garden spiders make sticky webs. Black widow spiders make tangled webs. Grass spiders make webs like little sheets.

Black Widow Spider

Some spiders hang nets of silk from corners or branches. Flying insects get tangled in the nets.

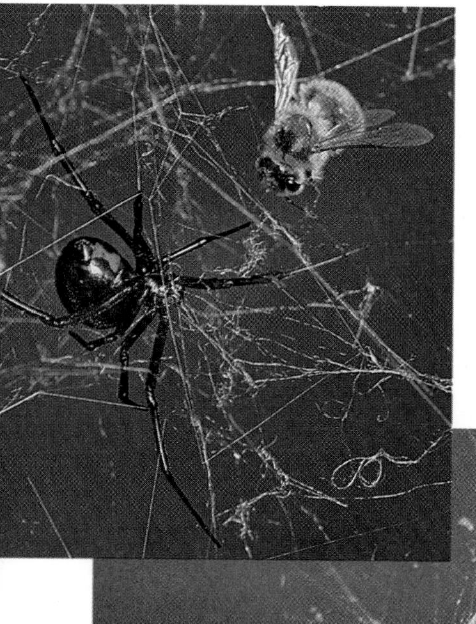

Some spiders dive into water and catch small fish and water insects.

Fisher Spider

Garden Spider

Some spiders fasten long, silk threads together like spokes of a wheel. They connect them with sticky threads on which insects get stuck. This kind of web is called an orb web.

An insect has six legs, wings, and feelers. But a spider has eight legs and no wings or feelers. A spider's skin is hard and covered with hair.

Wolf spiders and lynx spiders catch insects by chasing them. Jumping spiders catch insects by jumping on them.

Some spiders are fishermen. They wait by a stream or pond and catch water insects that swim past. Sometimes they dive into the water and grab fish. A raft spider makes a little boat of silk and leaves. When a small fish or water insect swims near the boat—the spider grabs it.

Spiders aren't insects. Insects have wings, feelers, and six legs. Spiders have no wings or feelers, and they have eight legs. Eight-legged animals are called arachnids.

Crab

Ten legs

Creeping over the sandy sea bottom is an animal that looks like a big insect. But it has ten legs. Two of the legs have big claws. The animal has long feelers. Its body is covered with a hard shell. It's a lobster.

Lobsters, crabs, shrimps, and barnacles are *crustaceans*. That's a word that means *animal with a crust*. Every part of a lobster's body is covered with a crust of hard skin, like armor.

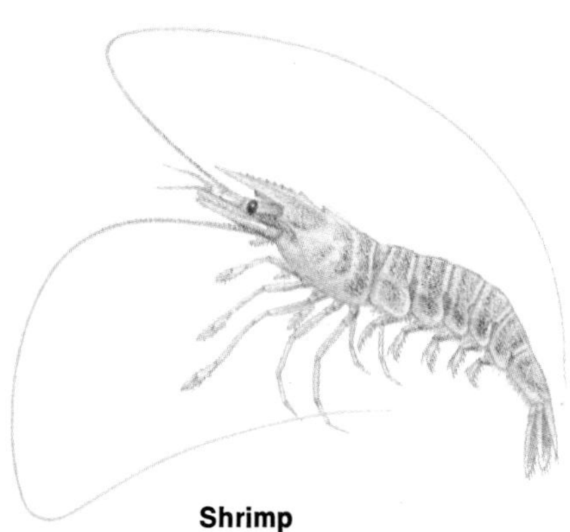

Shrimp

Crustaceans are cousins of the insects that fly and hop and creep about on land. But crustaceans are different from insects in several ways. Insects have six legs and two feelers. Crustaceans have at least ten legs, and four feelers. Insects breathe air through tiny holes in their bodies. Most crustaceans live in the water and breathe with gills, as fish do.

Crabs and lobsters look somewhat alike. But crabs have round, fat bodies. Lobsters have long bodies and wide, flat tails.

Shrimps are smaller than most crabs and lobsters. Some kinds of shrimps are so small they can be seen only with a microscope.

Barnacle

Barnacles are crustaceans that stop walking. When they are young they fasten themselves to rocks, floating pieces of wood, or the bottoms of ships. They are closed up inside their shells, with only their legs sticking out. They wiggle their legs to pull in tiny bits of food that float past in the water.

Lobsters, crabs, shrimps, and barnacles are cousins of the insects that live on land.

Lobster

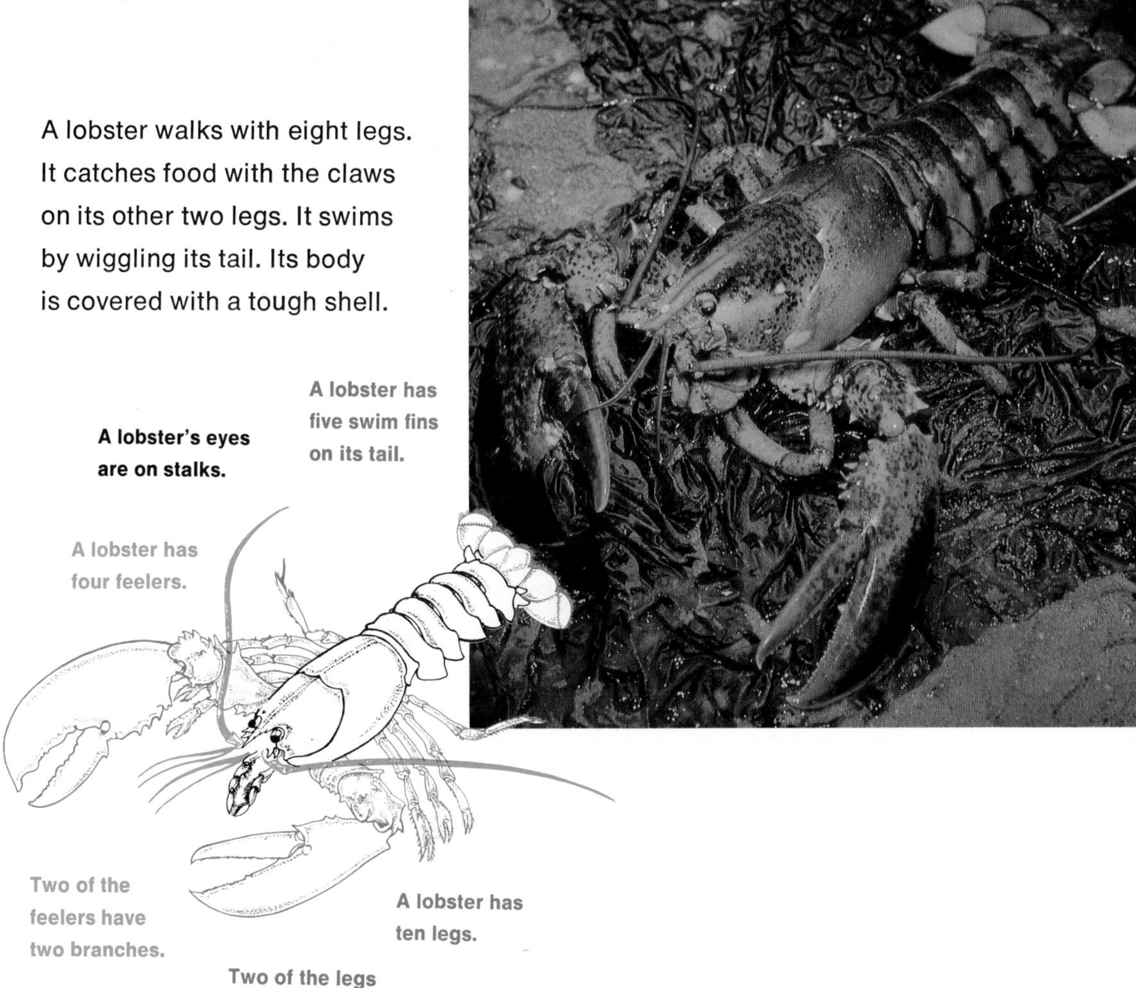

A lobster walks with eight legs. It catches food with the claws on its other two legs. It swims by wiggling its tail. Its body is covered with a tough shell.

The beauty of butterflies

Butterflies are very beautiful insects. Artists have painted butterflies, and poets have written about their beauty and grace for many years.

Butterflies come in many different sizes, colors, and patterns.

Peacock Butterfly

Scarce or Sail Swallowtail

Tropical Morpho Butterfly

Red Admiral Butterfly

Euthalia Ynipardus

Small Blues

A big change

A fat little brown and green caterpillar crawls on a leaf. A moth with beautiful black designs on its silver wings, flies past a bush. The moth and the caterpillar don't look a bit alike. But they are the same kind of animal. The caterpillar is a baby moth.

Every caterpillar you see in the summertime is a baby moth or butterfly. When a caterpillar comes out of its egg it spends a few weeks eating and growing. Then one day it's ready to change. Some caterpillars fasten themselves to tree trunks and cover themselves with silk that they make in their bodies. This silk covering is called a cocoon. Some caterpillars hang head down from tree branches. Their bodies become covered with hard shells. Some caterpillars dig into the ground.

Out of these little yellow balls will come tiny caterpillars. The caterpillars will eat and grow.

Puss Moth Eggs

A puss moth caterpillar looks like a twisted leaf. Its shape and color help it hide from enemies.

Puss Moth Caterpillar

The caterpillar goes to sleep in its cocoon, shell, or in the ground. Some caterpillars sleep during most of the summer and wake up in the fall. Some sleep during the winter and wake up in the spring. But when the caterpillar wakes from its long nap, it has changed.

It breaks out of its shell, or pushes out of its silk blanket, or crawls out of the ground. It isn't a short-legged caterpillar anymore. It has six long legs and two long feelers. Tiny raglike things on its back slowly swell up and become big wings. The crawling little caterpillar has become a flying creature—a moth or butterfly.

The caterpillar fastens itself to a twig. It covers itself with silk that it makes inside its body. It goes to sleep.

Puss Moth Cocoon

As it sleeps, the little caterpillar becomes a moth. It pushes out of the silk cocoon and flies away.

Puss Moth Adult

This grasshopper has grown too big for its baby skin. The skin dries and splits, and the grasshopper climbs out of it.

Changing skins

A young grasshopper climbs upon a twig. For a long time the grasshopper holds on to the twig without moving.

Then, a strange thing happens. The skin splits all along the grasshopper's back. Something pushes up out of the skin. It's the grasshopper. It is climbing out of its own skin!

All the many-legged creatures change skins many times during their lives. Insects, spiders, crabs, and lobsters all do it. For a few hours after changing skins, the new skins are soft. Then they turn hard like one of your fingernails.

In summer you may see what looks like a dead insect clinging to a twig or plant stem. It's an empty skin that an insect has grown out of and left behind.

The grasshopper's new wings are tiny and crumpled. As the grasshopper breathes, the wings fill with blood and stretch out.

The soft, new skin will become hard in a few hours. When the grasshopper grows too big, it will change skins again.

Grasshopper

Chirp, creak, buzz

Zeet-zeet-zeet!

Cree-cree-cree!

Ch-ch-ch-ch-urrrrr!

Those are some of the insect noises you can hear on a hot summer night.

Most of the chirps, creaks, and buzzes you hear are made by crickets, grasshoppers, katydids, and cicadas. The male insects make some of these noises to call to the female insects.

None of these insects makes its noise with its mouth. A male katydid makes its noise by rubbing its wings together. On one wing the katydid has a row of little teeth. On the other wing is a hard little scraper. When the scraper is rubbed over the teeth it makes the noise. You can make the same kind of noise by rubbing a pencil over the teeth of a comb.

Most insects make a buzzing noise when they fly. The noise is made by their wings moving up and down. Even so small an insect as a housefly makes a loud buzzing when it flies. But no insect has a voice. And although insects seem able to hear, most of them have no ears.

Grasshoppers, crickets, and katydids have ears, though. But the ears are in strange places. A grasshopper's ears are on its sides! And a katydid's ears are on its legs!

Katydid

This insect gets its name from the noise it makes. The noise sounds like "katy did-katy didn't-katy did-katy didn't."

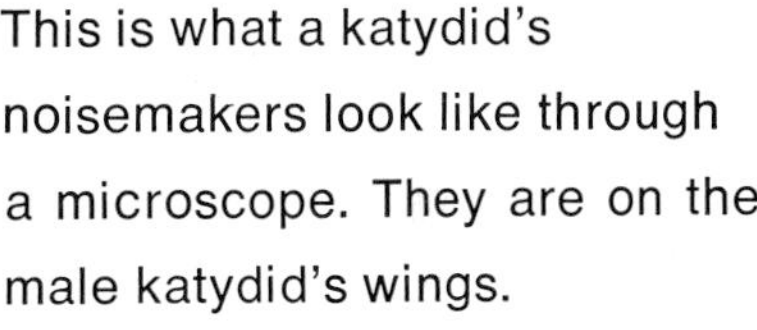

This is what a katydid's noisemakers look like through a microscope. They are on the male katydid's wings.

This is what a female katydid's leg looks like through a microscope. The hole is her ear.

Protection for insects

Insects are always in danger from many other animals. But many insects have ways of protecting themselves.

Many insects can fight back if they are attacked. Wasps, bees, hornets, and some other insects can give painful stings. Stink-bugs chase other insects away by spraying bad smells at them. The bombardier beetle shoots out a stinging, bad-tasting spray that will even chase frogs away.

Some insects are good at pretending to be something else. They don't do this on purpose, of course—they're just made that way. But when a katydid sits on a branch it

The bee's sting protects it.

Honeybee

Stinkbug

A bad smell protects this bug.

This insect's shape protects it.

Walking Stick

Monarch Butterfly

Viceroy Butterfly

looks like a leaf. Many kinds of moths look like pieces of tree bark. And walking sticks and some moth caterpillars look like twigs. Looking like something else is a good way for these insects to hide from other animals that might eat them.

Ladybugs, monarch butterflies, and some other insects taste bad. These insects are always brightly colored, usually orange and black. These colors say, "I taste bad!" Birds learn not to eat these insects. The insects are protected by their color.

But some insects that don't taste bad are colored orange and black, too. Birds are fooled by their colors and leave them alone. So those insects are protected by their colors, too.

Monarch butterflies taste bad to birds. Birds learn to tell monarch butterflies by their bright colors, and leave them alone. Viceroy butterflies don't taste bad. But they look much like monarch butterflies, so birds leave them alone, too. Both butterflies are protected by their bright colors.

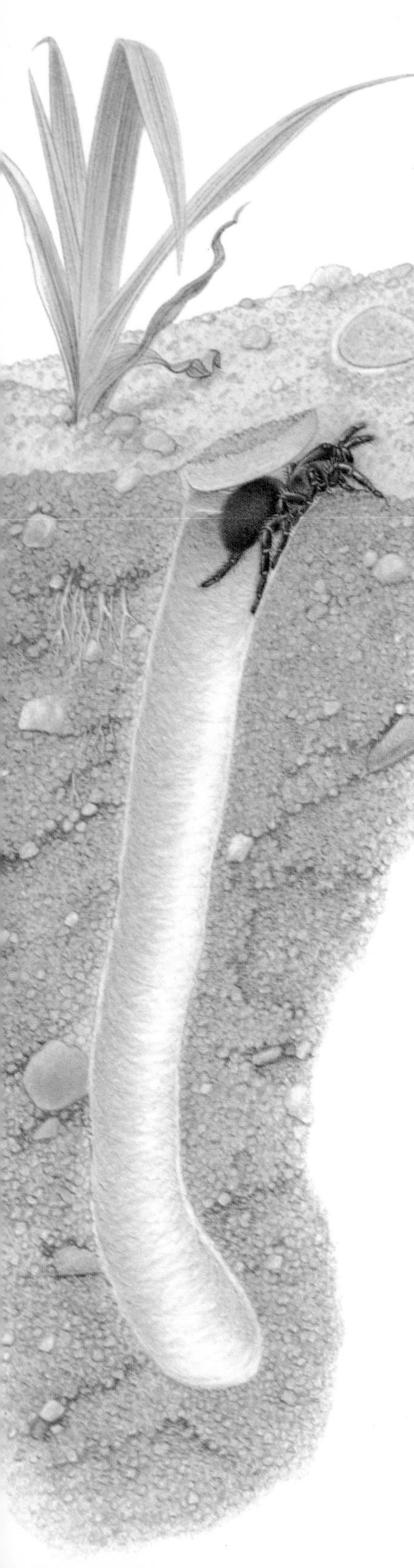

Many-legged home builders

In the sandy ground at the edge of a desert there is a small, round hole. Fastened to the hole is a little, round door. The door is open. What lives in this strange little house?

The hole in the sand is the doorway of a trap-door spider's home. The spider makes a long tunnel and lines it with silk. It

A trap-door spider's home is a silk-lined tunnel with a door made of silk and dirt.

Trap-Door Spider

Harvester ants live in tunnels that they dig in the ground.

Harvester Ants

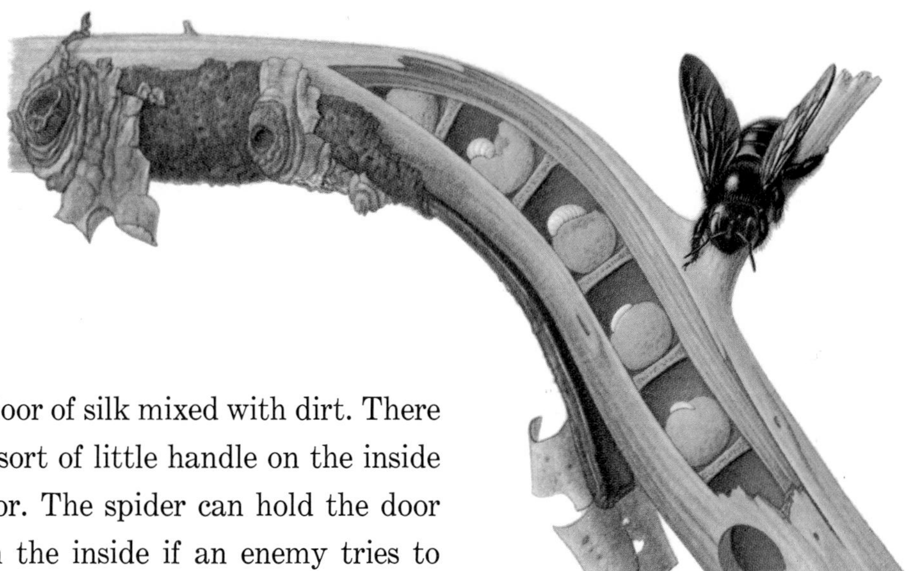

makes a door of silk mixed with dirt. There is even a sort of little handle on the inside of the door. The spider can hold the door shut from the inside if an enemy tries to get in.

Valley Carpenter Bee

The bee makes rooms inside a hollow stem. In each room is a white baby bee and a yellow ball of honey.

Lots of other many-legged animals make homes for themselves, too. The homes are made of silk, leaves, sand, dirt, and wood.

The purse web spider makes a long silk tube next to a tree trunk. The spider spends its whole life inside its long, round home.

The insect called a leaf roller makes itself a new house every day. It pulls a leaf around itself and fastens the edges together with silk that it makes in its body. Then it eats the inside of its house!

Many kinds of ants build whole cities. They dig tunnels and storerooms in dirt, sand, or wood. In some of the rooms they keep food, and in others they keep the queen ant's eggs.

One kind of termite makes a nest of dirt mixed with glue that comes from its body. The nests are taller than a man and harder than rock!

Paper Wasp

Some wasp nests are made of paper tubes. The wasps make the paper by chewing wood.

The flying fish lives in the sea.

The World of the Sea

Imagine an animal that has ten eyes, ten arms that shoot poison, and a body made of jelly! There really is such an animal. It's called a jellyfish and it lives in the sea.

The sea is filled with animals. It's the home of the frogfish and the eight-armed octopus. It's the home of the flying fish and the conch—a giant snail with a claw and a huge, twisted shell.

The sea is the home of animals that swim and float and creep, and of animals that fasten themselves down and never move again. It is the home of some of the tiniest of all animals and of the biggest animal that has ever lived.

The sea is a beautiful place. And it's a frightening place. It's a wonderland and a fairyland. It's another world!

The conch lives in the sea.

The octopus lives in the sea.

The frogfish lives in the sea.

Sea animals

The sea is filled with many kinds of animals. Fish, crabs, oysters, snails, and most other sea animals stay under water all the time. But whales, dolphins, sea turtles, sea snakes, and others breathe air. They must put their heads above water to breathe.

Many sea animals don't look like the kind of animal they really are. The eel looks like a snake, but it's a fish. Dolphins and whales look like fish, but they're not. They are mammals, like seals and walruses. And sponges, sea anemones, and corals don't even look like animals. They look like plants.

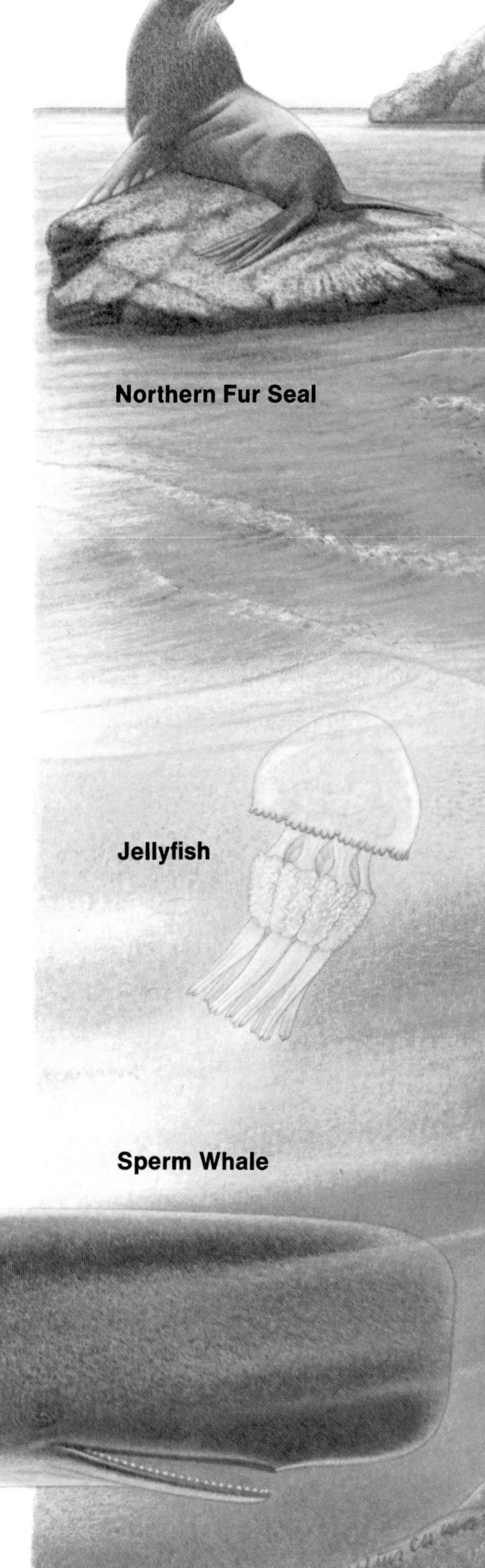

Northern Fur Seal

Jellyfish

Sperm Whale

Pacific Walrus
Bottle-Nosed Dolphin
Sardines
Elephant-Ear Sponge
Green Moray Eel
Green Crab
Pearl Oyster
Moon Snail

Meet the mollusks

Snails belong to a group of animals called mollusks. Mollusks have soft bodies with no bones. Some mollusks such as snails, clams, oysters, and scallops have outer shells for protection. Slugs, octopuses, and squids are mollusks that have no outer shells.

Mollusks live in most parts of the world. Land snails and slugs are two of the mollusks that live on land.

Land Snail

The land snail is a mollusk with a shell to protect its soft body.

Giant Clam

The giant clam lives between two shells. It can open and close its shells.

Others, such as octopuses, squid, and oysters, live in the seas and oceans. Freshwater clams and snails live in rivers, lakes, ponds, and streams. Wherever mollusks live, they must keep their bodies moist to stay alive. That's why slugs and some land snails can be found under damp leaves or in the soil.

The tongues of slugs and land snails are covered with tiny teeth. They use their tongues like files to eat leaves, fruit, and flowers.

Some mollusks live between two hinged shells that can open and close like a book. These animals are called bivalves. Clams, oysters, and scallops are bivalves. Bivalves usually keep their shells open just a little so that they can get food. They eat tiny plants and animals that float by in the water.

Living in a cup

An animal like a tiny flower floats down through the water of the sea. It fastens itself to the sandy bottom. It takes minerals out of the water and builds a tiny stone cup around itself.

After a while the little animal buds, just as a flower does. The bud grows and becomes another flower animal. The new animal builds a stone cup around itself. Then the new animal buds, too.

After many years, there is a big pile of the tiny stone cups, all stuck together. Inside each cup is one of the little flowerlike animals. During the day, each little animal hides inside its cup. At night, each animal stretches

Thousands of tiny animals that look like little flowers live in this lacy-looking coral.

Lace Coral

its body and holds out arms that look like flower petals. The arms catch tiny animals that swim near.

The stone cups stuck together are called coral. When a little flowerlike animal is inside each cup the coral looks like a field of flowers. The little animals are colored, so the coral may be red, pink, orange, blue, green, or purple. And different kinds of flowerlike animals put their cups together in different ways. The coral may be shaped like a bush, a fan, a round ball, or a bunch of lace.

Live coral is beautiful to see. It makes the world of the sea look like a fairyland.

Star Coral by Day

During the day, all the tiny coral animals are hiding inside their cups.

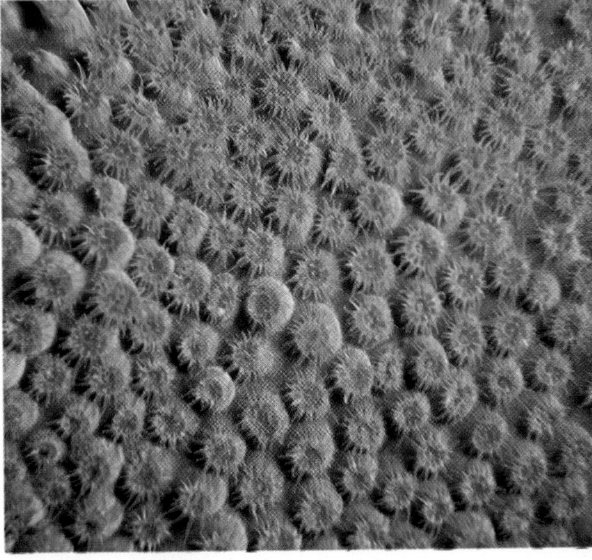

Star Coral at Night

At night, the coral animals come partway out. They spread their many arms to catch food.

Growing a new arm

There's an animal that has eyes and feet on its arms and turns its stomach inside out when it eats! And if it loses an arm—it grows a new one!

The animal is a starfish. Its body is shaped like a star. Each of the points of the star is an arm. Most starfish have five arms, but some have as many as fifty arms. On the underside of each arm are many tiny tubes. These are the starfish's feet. At the tip of each arm is a bunch of little

Sun Starfish

A starfish's points are its arms. Most starfish have five arms. Some have many more.

A starfish's feet are on the bottoms of its arms. The feet look like tiny tubes.

Common Starfish

A starfish pulls a clam's shell apart. Then the starfish puts its stomach into the shell and digests the clam.

Starfish and Clam

spots. These are the starfish's eyes. They can only see light and dark.

If a starfish has an arm bitten or torn off by another animal, the starfish can grow a new one. Sometimes an arm that has been torn off can grow a whole new starfish!

When a starfish finds a clam, oyster, or scallop it climbs onto it. The starfish pulls at each half of the clam or oyster shell. It pushes its stomach out through its mouth and slides it between the two halves of the shell. And it digests the clam or oyster right inside its own shell.

The pasture of the sea

Billions and billions of tiny plants and animals live in the ocean. Most of them are so small they can be seen only with a microscope.

These tiny plants aren't like plants you have seen. Some look like squares of jelly fastened together in chains. Some look like little balls. Some are like tiny anchors with threads hanging from them.

The tiny animals are strange looking, too. Some look like bells. Some look like light bulbs with six wiggly legs. Some of them are just little round balls. Many of these animals are the babies of bigger animals, such as jellyfish.

All these plants and animals float in the upper part of the ocean. They are called plankton. Plankton is the most important food in the sea. It is often called the pasture of the sea.

Many kinds of baby fish eat plankton. So do many grown fish. So do many other sea animals. If suddenly there were no plankton, all these animals would die. And all the animals that eat them for food would then die. Soon there wouldn't be a single living thing in any of the oceans.

That's why plankton is the most important food in the sea.

Billions of tiny plants and animals float in the ocean. They are called plankton. They are the food of many of the big animals in the ocean. This is what plankton looks like through a microscope.

Plankton

Biggest of all!

What is the biggest animal that has ever lived?

It's not one of the giant dinosaurs of long ago. It's an animal that is living right now. It is the blue whale.

A blue whale is so long and wide that five elephants in a row could stand on its back.

Whales look like big fish. But whales aren't fish. They are mammals. They spend all their lives in water, but they breathe air, just as we do. If a whale stays underwater too long, it drowns.

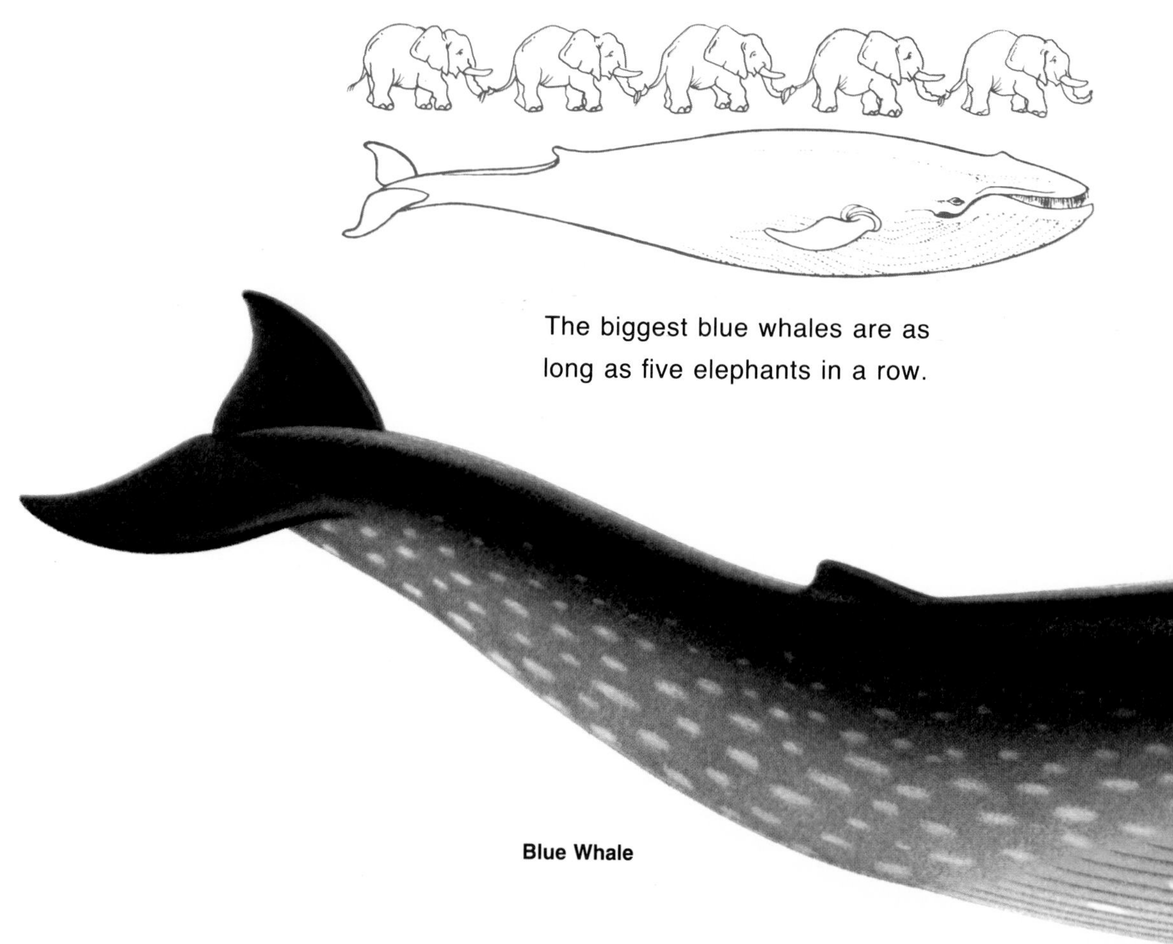

The biggest blue whales are as long as five elephants in a row.

Blue Whale

It seems as if big whales should eat big things. But some of the biggest of all animals eat the smallest things in the ocean. Blue whales, right whales, bowheads, and finbacks eat plankton. Plankton is made up of plants and animals so tiny you can't see them without a microscope.

Other whales are meat-eaters. Narwhals and bottlenoses eat fish, crabs, and lobsters. Sperm whales eat fish, too. But a sperm whale's favorite food is giant squid. Killer whales eat seals and porpoises.

Once, there were many whales in the seas. But men have hunted whales for many years. The whales are killed for meat and oil. Now there aren't many whales left. The big blue whales have almost all been killed. The biggest animal that ever lived may soon be gone forever.

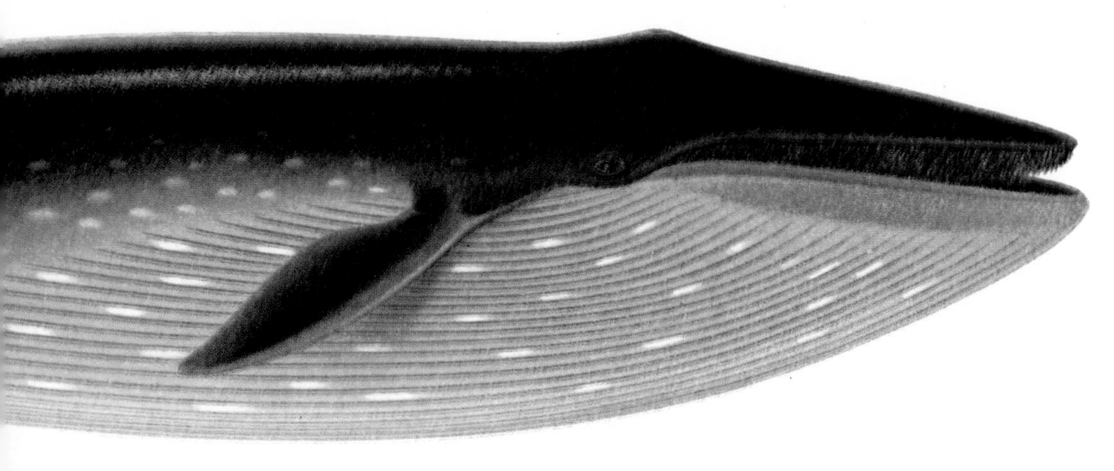

Sea Peaches

The sea peach is one kind of sea squirt. Sea squirts suck water in, then squirt it out.

To eat, a sea cucumber slides its arms through the sand or mud, puts them into its mouth and sucks the mud off them!

Sea Cucumber

Sea peaches, cucumbers, grapes

You would never find a sea peach in a basket of fruit, or a sea cucumber in a salad. Because a sea peach isn't a fruit and a sea cucumber isn't a vegetable. They're animals!

Sea peaches belong to the family of animals called sea squirts. Most kinds of sea squirts are just round bodies with two openings like little mouths. One mouth sucks water in. The other mouth squirts water out. The sea squirt eats the tiny animals and bits of plants in the water it sucks in.

Sea squirts stay fastened to the rocks or sand and never move. But sea cucumbers crawl slowly over the sand and mud. They crawl on many feet that look like little tubes.

A sea cucumber has a long, round body with what looks like a bunch of leaves at one end. These are the sea cucumber's "fingers." It eats by sucking food off them just as you might lick jelly from your fingers. As the sea cucumber crawls, it rubs its "fingers" in the sand or mud. Bits of food stick to them. Then the sea cucumber puts them in its mouth, one at a time, and cleans them.

The sea peach and sea cucumber aren't the only sea animals that look like other things. The sea urchin looks like a round pincushion with pins sticking out all over it. The sea grape is a little sea squirt that looks like a green grape. And the sand dollar is an animal that looks like a cooky!

Sea Urchin

A sea urchin's round body is covered with spikes. Some sea urchins' spikes are poisonous.

This looks like a cooky, but it's a sea animal that moves about on many feet that look like tiny tubes.

Sand Dollar

A porcupine's quills help it stay alive.

Staying Alive

Far up near the North Pole a tiny, baby seal lies in the snow. If a polar bear saw the baby seal, the bear would eat it up in a minute!

But the polar bear cannot see the baby seal. The seal's stiff, white fur is the same color as the snow. The baby seal is protected by its color.

Most animals need some kind of protection to keep from being eaten. Some animals are protected by their shape or color, like the baby seal. Some animals are protected by armor. Some are good fighters. Some are fast runners.

But whether it runs or fights or hides, nearly every animal must have some way of protecting itself—to stay alive!

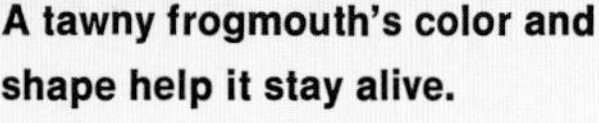

A tawny frogmouth's color and shape help it stay alive.

A gazelle's speed helps it stay alive.

A seal pup's color
helps it stay alive.

Hiding with color

Hop! A green grasshopper shoots up out of the grass. It sails through the air and lands in the grass again. You can't see it before it jumps. And you can't see it after it comes down. Its green color helps it hide in the green grass.

An animal is hard to see if it is the same color as the ground, rocks, or plants around it. A green caterpillar on a green leaf is hard to see, and so is a brown horned toad on brown sand. The caterpillar's color helps it hide from birds while it is eating. The horned toad's color helps it hide from birds and snakes while it looks for insects to eat.

The spots and stripes that many animals have on their bodies help them hide, too. A giraffe's body is pale orange or white, with reddish-brown spots. When the giraffe walks among trees it seems to disappear. Its spotted body looks like spots of sunlight and shadow among the leaves.

A tiger's coat is orange-brown with black stripes. When the tiger lies in a field of brown grass striped with sun and shadow, it can't be seen. When another animal comes near enough, the tiger can jump out of hiding at it.

The color and designs on an animal's body help it hide so it can get food—or so it can keep from becoming food!

Giraffe

The colors and designs on a giraffe's body help the giraffe hide when it stands among the trees.

Tomato Hornworm

A hungry bird may not be able to see a green caterpillar on a green leaf.

Pheasant

The colors of a pheasant's feathers make it look like a pile of leaves.

Changing color

How would you like to play hide-and-seek with a chameleon?

You'd have a hard time finding this tiny lizard. It can hide by changing color! It can be green on a green leaf, yellow on yellow sand, and gray on a gray rock.

The kind of shrimp called a prawn is an even better color changer than a chameleon. The prawn can be green when it swims among green seaweed, orange when it is near orange coral, and brown on brown rocks. At night, when the water is dark blue, the prawn turns blue, too.

A champion color changer is the fish called a sole. It can turn yellow, brown, blue, green, and even pink. It can even turn more than one color at a time. If it lies on brown sand that has little yellow stones in it, the sole's body turns brown with yellow spots! Scientists once put a sole into a tank that had a polka dot design on the bottom. The sole's body turned polka-dotted!

How do these animals change color? Under the animal's skin are many tiny, tiny sacs filled with color. Tubes like little tree branches reach up from the sacs to the skin. Different kinds of light on the animal's skin make the tubes fill up with color, and this colors the skin.

An animal that can change color is lucky. It can stay hidden wherever it goes.

Sole

Soles, and some other fish, can change color to match the sand over which they swim. This sole has taken on a pink tint as it swims over pink sand.

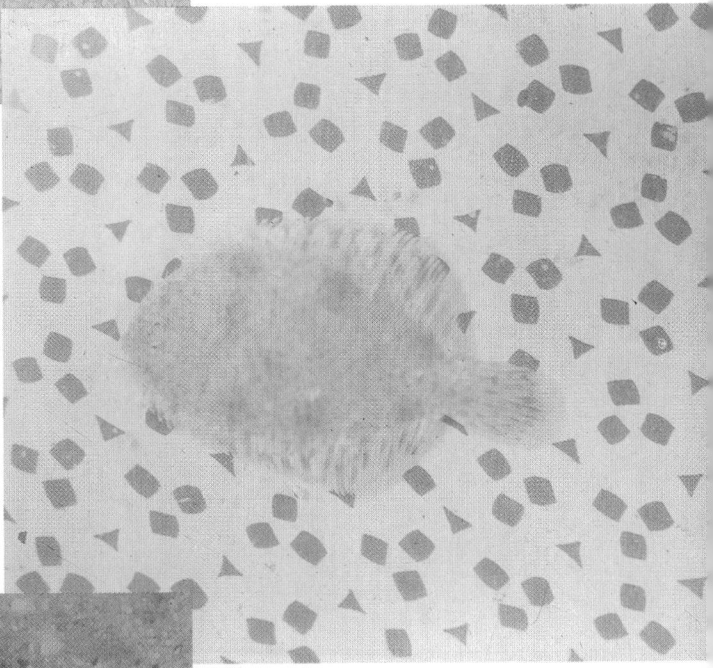

Scientists put this sole into a tank with a speckled bottom. The sole wasn't able to match the color and speckles very well.

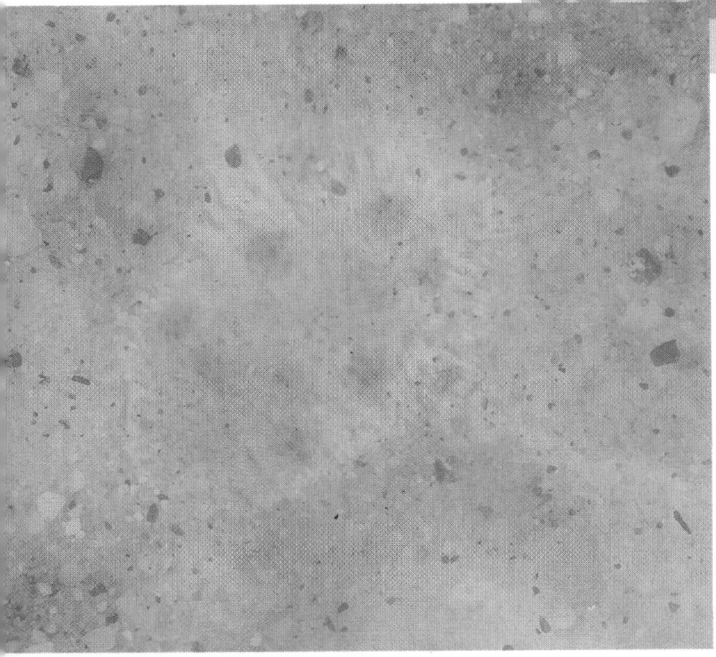

The sole has matched the color of this yellow sand so well that it is nearly invisible.

Animal actors

Many animals protect themselves by pretending.

The frilled lizard is small and harmless. But it pretends to be big and dangerous. When it opens its mouth its throat is bright red and frightening. A big flap of skin on its neck lifts up and spreads out. The lizard suddenly looks much bigger and very dangerous!

The harmless hog-nose snake pretends to be dangerous, too. It opens its mouth and hisses. It pretends it's going to bite. But then, if its enemy isn't frightened, the hog-nose snake acts dead. It rolls over onto its back and lies still. Most animals don't care to eat dead snakes, so the enemy usually goes away.

Some animals pretend that they aren't even animals. The bird called a tawny frogmouth pretends to be part of a tree. Its feathers look like bark. It sits on a branch,

This frightened snake is pretending to be dead so that its enemy will go away.

Eastern Hognose Snake

Frilled Lizard

The frilled lizard looks frightening, but it is really harmless.

stretches itself out, and closes its eyes. It looks just like a broken branch.

Some animal actors have disguises that protect them from enemies and help them get food at the same time. The South American leaf fish looks just like a leaf floating in the water. Bigger fish pass right by it. But when a smaller fish swims near—*gulp!* The leaf fish swallows it down!

These animal actors don't know they're pretending. It's just one of the ways they stay alive.

Animals in armor

If you saw a pangolin you might say it looked like a pine cone with legs and a tail.

A pangolin is one of the animals that is protected by armor. It's covered with scales like the scales on a pine cone, only bigger. When a pangolin is frightened it rolls itself into a ball. It tucks its head between its legs and covers its stomach with its tail. Its sharp-edged scales stick up. Not even a tiger would care to try to bite through them.

The armadillo is another animal in armor. In fact, the word *armadillo* means *little armored thing*. Armadillos are born with soft skin. But as they grow, their skins become covered with small, flat pieces of bone. This bony armor covers an armadillo's back, sides, head, tail, and the insides of its legs. The armadillo protects itself by rolling into a ball as the pangolin does. Then it's a hard, bony ball that a wolf or bobcat finds hard to bite.

Pangolin

Hedgehog

(above) Hedgehogs are protected by a covering of sharp stickers, or spines. (right) Armadillos can't fight well. They need their armor to protect them from animals that might eat them.

Nine-Banded Armadillo

Porcupines, hedgehogs, porcupine fish, and sea urchins wear a sort of armor, too. Their bodies are covered with sharp stickers that keep other animals from biting them.

Pangolins, armadillos, porcupines, hedgehogs, and sea urchins can't run fast, hide, or fight well. Wearing armor helps them stay alive.

Lioness Hunting Wildebeests

A lion hunts by sneaking up close to its prey and then rushing at it. The lioness does most of the hunting for lion families.

A race for life

When you run in a race, it's just for fun. But many kinds of animals run in races that often mean life or death for one of them.

When a lion hunts a wildebeest it tries to creep as close as it can. If the lion gets close enough, it can jump on the wildebeest's back and kill it. But if the wildebeest sees or smells the lion, it dashes away. Then the race begins!

Both animals run for their lives. The lion must catch the wildebeest so it can eat. The wildebeest must escape so it can go on living. If the wildebeest gets a quick start, or if the lion is old and slow, the wildebeest may get away. But if the lion is young and fast it will probably catch the wildebeest and kill it.

Animals that get their food by chasing other animals are fast runners. A person could never win a race against them. Foxes and wolves can run about twice as fast as a person. And a cheetah can run at least three times as fast as a person. It's the fastest of all land animals.

The kinds of animals that lions, wolves, and other hunting animals eat are fast runners, too. Gazelles can run faster than race horses. Jack rabbits and zebras are nearly as fast as gazelles. Even big, clumsy-looking giraffes can run much faster than a person.

Lions, leopards, and cheetahs chase antelopes, wildebeests, and zebras. Wolves chase deer and elk. Coyotes and foxes chase rabbits. The hunter runs so it can eat. The animal it chases runs to keep from being eaten. The animal that wins the race is the one that stays alive.

Tooth and claw

The sun is setting on the cactus and sagebrush of a desert in North America. A badger is busily digging beside a bush.

Along comes a coyote. It sees the badger and licks its lips with a long, pink tongue. The coyote is planning to have a badger supper.

The badger tries to run. But the coyote dashes toward it and heads it off. The badger is trapped.

But suddenly the badger snarls, showing its sharp teeth! It rushes at the coyote and strikes at it with sharp claws!

The coyote jumps back. It is much bigger than the badger, but it doesn't like the looks of the badger's teeth and claws. The coyote trots off to find an easier supper. The badger has saved its life by fighting back.

The badger is a good fighter. But even animals that seem harmless will often fight to keep from being eaten. Zebras, giraffes, and deer kick with their hard, sharp hoofs. They can make deep, terrible cuts on an enemy. The harmless-looking ostrich defends itself by kicking, too. A kick from one of its big feet can break a hyena's back! When the giant anteater is in danger it stands up on its back legs and fights with the sharp claws on its front legs.

An animal uses whatever weapons it has when it is fighting for its life.

Coyote and Badger

The coyote would like to eat the badger, but it's afraid. The badger is a good fighter and will defend itself.

Animal Ways

A harvester ant goes to work every day.

Why do birds sing? Why do ants rush about so busily? Why does a mandrill sometimes seem to yawn when it sees another animal? Are there reasons for what the animals do?

Animals cannot think as people can. But there is nearly always a reason for the things animals do. A bird's song may be a warning of danger, a threat, or an invitation to a mate. Ants rush about to find food they can bring back to the nest. And the mandrill isn't yawning—he's warning the other animal not to come near or he'll fight!

Animals do things to protect themselves, to find food, or to be more comfortable. And sometimes they even do things just for fun.

A chaffinch's song can be a warning.

Sometimes a mandrill's yawn means "Keep away!"

African Elephants

A mother elephant protects her baby
by keeping it between her legs.
If the mother sees an enemy, she lifts
her trunk and makes a warning noise.

Protecting the babies

Snow whirls through the air. The wind howls. There's a blizzard coming to the icy land around the South Pole. That's where the emperor penguins live. The grown-up penguins hurry about, pushing all the baby penguins together. Then the grown-ups crowd together in a tight circle around the babies. This is how the grown-up penguins protect the babies from a storm.

In Africa, a mother elephant and her baby trot across a hot, grassy plain. The mother keeps the baby between her legs as she walks. This is how she protects it from animals that might try to kill it. If the mother sees an animal that might be an enemy, she raises her trunk. She makes a loud screaming noise. This warns the animal not to come too close!

Three brand-new baby herons lie in a nest in North America. The mother heron stands on the nest and fans the babies with her wings. The babies will die if they get too hot, so the mother heron keeps them cool.

Baby animals are in danger from many things. Many of them would die or be killed if they weren't protected. But many kinds of grown-up animals protect their babies from all the things that might harm them.

Sounds that say things

Red-Winged Blackbird

When a male bird sings in the springtime he is often telling other male birds to stay away.

Owls hoot. Foxes yap. Crickets chirp. Geese honk. Chipmunks chatter. And many of these animal sounds mean something.

Some animal noises are warnings. In the spring a male red-winged blackbird sings, *"Cock-a-ree!"* This is a warning to other male blackbirds. It means, "This is my place! Stay away or I'll fight you!"

Some animal noises are invitations. The tiny frogs called spring peepers make a noise that sounds like sleigh bells. The noise is made by male frogs to invite female frogs to come to them.

Some sounds are calls for help. A dolphin that is hurt or in trouble makes a high, whistling noise. Then other dolphins come to help it.

Some sounds mean "Danger!" If the bird called a chaffinch sees a hawk in the sky the chaffinch sings, *"Seet! Seet!"* Other chaffinches quickly hide in trees and bushes where the hawk can't see them.

Animal noises aren't words. Animals can't talk, as we do. But many sounds that animals make really do say something.

Coyote

When a coyote howls, others usually begin to howl, too. Some people think that coyote howls are signals.

When a beaver fears danger it slaps the water with its tail. This makes a big splash and a loud noise. The noise warns other beavers of danger. When they hear it, they hurry into the water and swim away.

Beaver

A long winter nap

In the autumn, a woodchuck curls up into a ball in its underground home and goes to sleep. And it sleeps during the whole winter.

The woodchuck's sleep isn't like the sleep you have at night. The woodchuck's heart slows down and nearly stops. The woodchuck's breathing nearly stops, too. And the woodchuck's body changes. Most of the time the woodchuck's body is warm because it is a warm-blooded animal. But the woodchuck's body grows cold before it goes into its winter sleep.

The woodchuck's sleep is called hibernation. Ground squirrels, bats, and some other warm-blooded animals also hibernate in the same way. Bears hibernate too, but their bodies do not get as cold as do the bodies of the smaller animals.

Snakes, turtles, frogs, and toads also hibernate, but in a different way. A snake is cold-blooded. Its body is always just as warm or cold as the air around it. So as the weather grows colder a snake's body grows colder. The snake tries to get warm by crawling into a hole. The weather gets colder and the snake's body gets colder and stiff. Its heart and breathing nearly stop.

The snake must wait until warm weather comes before its body warms up enough so that it can move. But the woodchuck's body warms up by itself, long before warm weather comes. There's often snow still on the ground when the woodchuck wakes up and scampers out of its hole.

Woodchuck

A woodchuck sleeps all winter in its underground home. This kind of long sleep is called hibernation.

In winter a snake's body gets so cold and stiff it can't move until warm weather comes. This is a kind of hibernation, too.

Water Snake

Migrating Birds

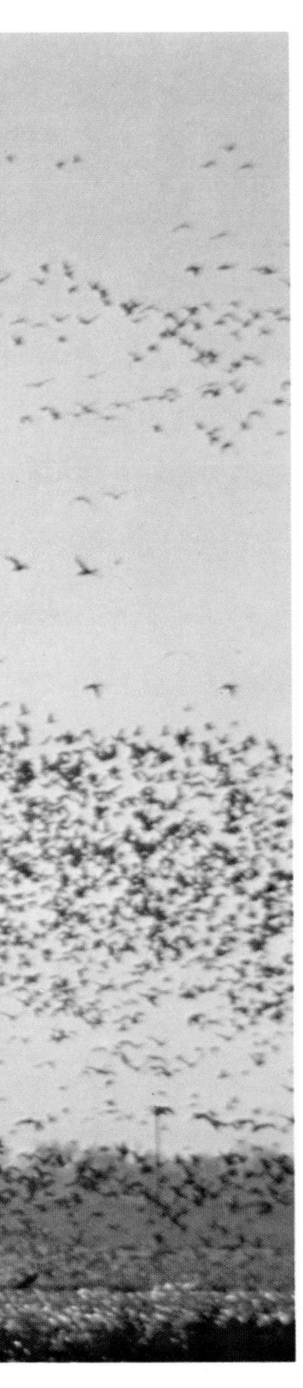

The great mystery

Hundreds of barn swallows sit in rows on telephone wires. Suddenly, with a great twittering, they all rush into the air. Staying close together in a big flock, they fly away. It is late summer and the barn swallows have begun to migrate.

Every autumn millions of geese, ducks, storks, cuckoos, bobolinks, and other birds migrate. They leave the north, where they spent the summer, and fly south. Sometimes many birds fly together. Some birds fly alone.

When birds migrate they often fly great distances. Sometimes they cross oceans and continents. But the birds always go to the same warm parts of the world where their ancestors have gone for thousands of years. The birds stay all winter in these warm places. In the spring they migrate back to the north. Sometimes they go back to the same nests they used the summer before.

Birds aren't the only animals that migrate. Monarch butterflies, ladybugs, and many other insects migrate, too. So do some fish and mammals.

It is usually still warm when birds and insects begin to migrate. How do they know winter is coming? How do they know where to go? What makes them always go to the same place?

Scientists know that something in a bird's or insect's body makes it leave at the right time and steers it the way it should go. But no one is sure of all the causes. Migration is a great mystery!

Helpful animals

Crocodiles try to eat most birds that come near them. But one kind of bird can walk about among crocodiles and be quite safe. In fact, these birds even lay their eggs in the same place where the crocodiles lay their eggs!

The birds are called water dikkops and they eat insects that bother the crocodiles. Of course, this gives the birds an easy meal, but it also makes the crocodiles more comfortable. So the birds are really helping the crocodiles and maybe that's why the crocodiles don't harm them.

Other birds, called tickbirds, help the rhinoceros. A rhinoceros usually won't let other kinds of animals near it. But it lets tickbirds ride on its back! Tiny insects on the rhinoceros' back bite it and make it itch, and the tickbird eats these insects. This makes the rhinoceros feel better.

Little fish called wrasses help many other fish. Tiny worms often fasten themselves to a fish and make sores on its body. When this happens the fish goes to a coral reef where a wrasse lives. The little wrasse hunts all over the fish's body and eats all the worms.

The water dikkop, the tickbird, and the wrasse are all getting something from the animals they help. They are getting food. And the animals they help are getting rid of pests that bother them and cause them pain. Scientists call this mutualism.

Tickbirds and Black Rhinoceros

The tickbirds help the rhinoceros by eating insects that bother it.

The little cleaner fish are helping the big fish by eating tiny worms that are on it.

Cleaner Fish

Safety in numbers

A herd of baboons hunts for food at the edge of a grassy plain in Africa. Each baboon is looking and listening every second. There might be a lion creeping through the grass toward them!

If a baboon sees or hears something, it gives a loud grunt. It sounds almost like a man yelling "Hah!" Then all the baboons hurry to climb trees. Because of one baboon's warning, all the baboons are safe.

Some animals live together in herds. They are safer that way. An animal by itself may not see or hear the enemy that creeps toward it. But if there are many animals together, there are many more chances that one animal will see or smell danger and warn the others.

Baboons

Musk Oxen and Wolves

When the musk oxen are in a circle, wolves don't dare attack.

Herds of baboons, zebras, antelopes, and deer run when they are warned of danger. But sometimes a whole herd of animals will fight an enemy.

When big, shaggy musk oxen in Canada are attacked by wolves, the musk oxen quickly get into a circle with the babies on the inside. The musk oxen stand with their big heads down. Their sharp horns point out at the wolves. The wolves snarl and growl but they don't dare attack. As long as the musk oxen stay in their circle the whole herd is safe.

Sometimes one animal by itself isn't as safe as it is in a herd. There's safety in numbers!

A wood-ant city

An ant nest is like a little city where hundreds or even thousands of ants live together. Ants make their nests by digging tunnels and storerooms in the ground.

The picture on the page across from this one shows a wood-ant nest. If you look at the picture carefully, you can see a lot going on. On the ground above the nest a group of workers hunts for food. The ant with wings is a male. Male ants don't do any work.

Inside the nest, in the top tunnel, two workers are bringing in part of a leaf. They will use it to repair the nest. Other workers are getting ready to carry cocoons to another room. Inside each cocoon is a baby ant. When the babies grow up they will break out of the cocoons and go right to work.

In the next tunnel is the queen ant. She is much bigger than the workers. She spends her whole life laying eggs. She is the mother of all the ants in the nest.

Ants work together as if they were quite smart. But they aren't really smart. They can't think about things as you can. An ant does things because its body gets signals, such as smells. Different smells make ants do different things.

Ants never change or learn anything new. They can't. Hundreds of millions of years ago ants were living the same way and doing the same sort of things they do now.

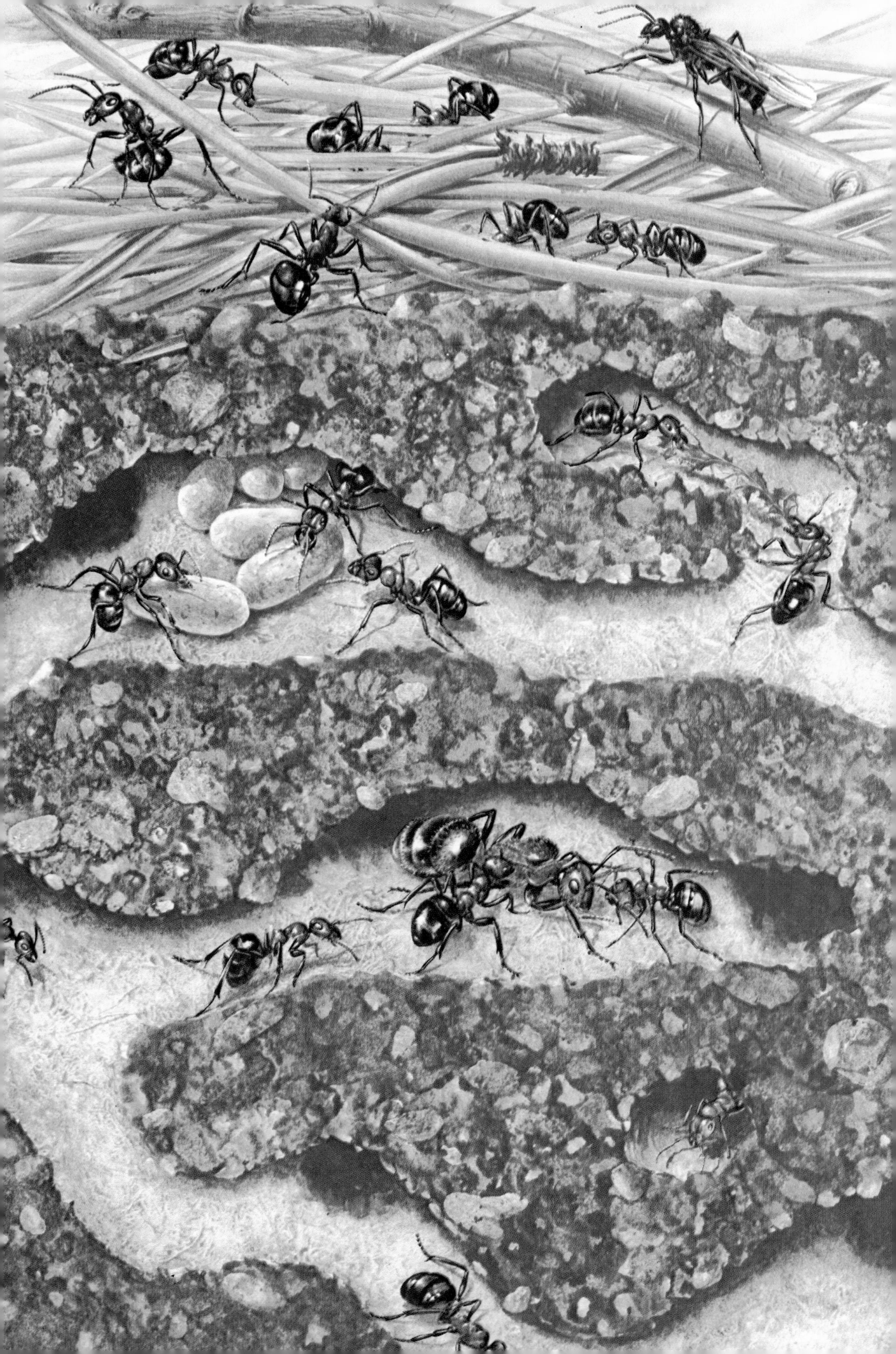

Fox Pups

These fox pups are playing, but they are also practicing the hunting skills they will use when they are grown.

Animal games

Do you like to play tag? So do chimpanzees.

Chimpanzees chase each other in and out among trees and bushes, screaming and chattering. They look as if they're angry but they're really having fun. Sometimes, as if to start a game, a young chimpanzee pinches another and runs away!

Seals love to play, too. They snort and bark and splash and play tag in the water.

Chimpanzees, seals, and many other animals seem to play just for fun, as you do. But when many baby animals play, they are learning things at the same time. They are exercising their bodies and learning how to hunt.

Wolf cubs play by rushing at each other. They snap and growl and try to knock each other down. When they are older, they hunt by running after other animals and trying to knock them down.

Fox pups learn by playing, too. When one is lying down, another will creep slowly toward it and jump on its tail. When they are grown, foxes get food the same way, by creeping toward an animal and jumping upon it.

Many baby mammals play for fun and to learn things. But baby insects, reptiles, amphibians, and fish never seem to play. They are too busy trying to find food and trying to keep from being eaten.

A painted lady butterfly smells its world through its feelers.

The Animals' World

We see, hear, smell, and feel the world around us. So do animals. But many animals do these things in different ways. Some kinds of animals can't do all of them. Some kinds of animals do them better than others.

So, for each kind of animal, the world is different. Some animals see colors, other animals see only shades of gray. For some animals the world is filled with smells, for others there are no smells at all. Some animals can't hear. Some can't see at all.

For some kinds of animals the world is *very* different. A bat's world is darkness filled with echoing sound. For a butterfly the world is filled with shapes and colors and smells we can hardly imagine.

But each kind of animal has exactly the right kind of eyes, or nose, or ears, or feelers, or tail, or other things it needs to find its way and live its life in its world.

To a fennec fox, the world is filled with sounds.

A woolly monkey's tail helps it live in its treetop world.

The great horned owl's big eyes can see clearly in the dark.

What animals see

A hawk can see much better than a person can. From high in the sky, a hawk can see a tiny mouse in the grass below.

Broadwinged Hawk

If you were a rabbit, nibbling plants in a meadow, you would be able to see in front, on both sides, and nearly all the way behind—all at the same time!

But you wouldn't see any color at all. Everything would be gray and fuzzy, like a black-and-white TV picture that isn't tuned in just right. But if something moved

behind you, you would see the movement at once.

If you were a hawk, you would see things in colors, just as people do. But your eyes would be like magnifying glasses. A hawk flying at 1,000 feet (300 meters) can see a mouse in the grass.

If you could see through a bee's eyes things would look most strange to you. A field of red flowers would seem like a big, black shadow. Yellow daisies would have glowing spots that people can't see. The glowing spots are a color called ultraviolet. Bees see ultraviolet, but people cannot.

Many other animals see things very differently from the way people do. Some spiders have eight eyes! What do you suppose things look like to them? How do things look to a lobster or an octopus? We can only guess. But each kind of animal sees the way it must, to stay alive.

These are pictures of the same flower. The bottom picture was taken with a special kind of light. It shows that there's a color we can't see in the middle of the flower. A bee sees this color as a bright glow.

Deer

Because a deer's eyes are on the sides of its head, a deer can see in front, on both sides, and partway behind itself all at the same time.

Horseshoe Bat

Listen!

A bat flies through a cave. Long, sharp rocks hang from the roof. Other rocks stick up from the floor. The cave is darker than night. If you were there, you wouldn't see a thing. But the flying bat doesn't bump into a single rock.

How does the bat tell where the rocks are? It hears them!

As the bat flies, it makes tiny squeaks. If a rock is ahead of the bat, the squeak bounces off the rock and makes an echo. The bat hears the echo and knows something is there. The bat flies around the rock.

A bat's ears can hear sounds that you can't. If you were in the cave with the bat, you wouldn't hear either the bat's squeaks or the echo.

Birds can hear better than humans, too. Have you ever seen a thrush or a blackbird stand with its head to one side? It's listening to a worm crawl. The bird hops toward the noise and pulls the worm from its hole. A bird's ears are two little holes, one on each side of its head.

Deer, big-eared rabbits, and many other animals need good hearing to keep from being eaten. They can move their ears to listen for the tiny noises that may mean a wolf, bobcat, or other enemy is near. Then they can run away or hide from the enemy.

Dogs can turn the open part of their ears to the direction a sound is coming from. This dog is not hearing anything special.

Someone is saying the dog's name very softly. The dog's head does not turn. The dog's ears move to catch the sound.

A world of smells

The squirrel can tell if the hickory nut is good or bad by the way it smells.

Flying Squirrel

Even though you can't see them, you can tell when cookies are baking nearby. You can't see perfume on a lady, but you can tell she's wearing it. And you know if someone has been eating peppermint if they stand close to you. Your nose tells you all these things.

An animal's nose tells it many things, too. In fact, most animals' noses tell them a lot more than your nose tells you. A squirrel sniffs at a nut before carrying the nut home. If you sniffed at the nut you

With its two feathery, golden feelers, this moth can smell another moth that is far away.

Luna Moth

When a snake pokes its tongue out it is smelling. A snake's tongue helps it smell things.

Israeli Racer

might not smell anything at all. But the squirrel's nose tells the squirrel if the nut is good or rotten.

When a snake goes hunting it pokes its Y-shaped tongue in and out. A snake's tongue can find the smell of a mouse or frog even in a whole forest of other smells. The snake follows the smell by sticking its tongue in and out.

Insects can smell things very well even though they have no noses. An insect smells with its two wiggly feelers. A male luna moth has feelers like two golden feathers. These feelers can smell a female luna moth a mile (1.6 kilometers) away!

Smell helps an animal find food or find a mate. Smell lets an animal know that an enemy is near. Each animal lives in its own world of smells—and every smell means something to it.

A different way of hunting

A hungry rattlesnake glides through the grass at night. The animals it hunts can't see it well in the dark. The snake can't see them either, but it doesn't have to. It has another way of finding them.

On the rattlesnake's head, just below its eyes, are two openings called pits. These pits can feel the warmth of another animal's body—even though the animal is not very near.

Suddenly, the snake turns to the left. A rat is nearby and the rattlesnake's pits have felt the heat of the rat's warm body. Silently the snake moves closer. Then it shoots its head forward and catches the rat in its mouth. The snake's pits guided the snake right to where the rat was!

Below each eye on a rattlesnake's head is a hole called a pit. The rattlesnake's pits help it find the animals it eats.

Banded Rattlesnake and Wood Rat

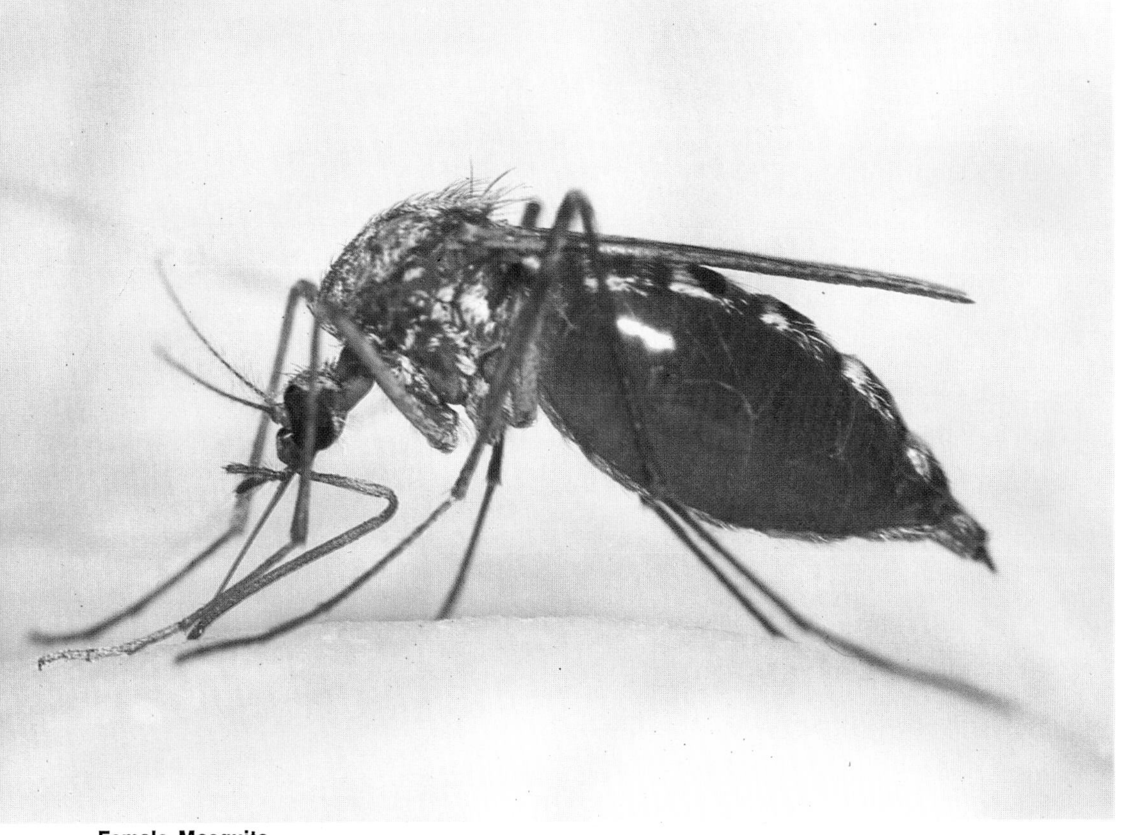

Female Mosquito

On a female mosquito's round, knoblike head are two feelers that help her find her food.

A female mosquito can feel warmth a long way off, too. She feels heat with her two wiggly feelers. The blood of warm animals is a female mosquito's food. When a mosquito comes onto your arm, her feelers have told her you were warm—and she wants to eat!

We know what it's like for an animal to hunt by seeing, hearing, and smelling. But what would it be like to hunt by feeling an animal's warmth a long way off, as rattlesnakes and mosquitoes do? That's part of the world of animals that we can only imagine.

The night world

A mouse scampers through the grass in a meadow. It is night and only the stars are out. The mouse can hardly see, but it finds its way in the dark, because it is in its territory. The air is full of smells, and the mouse sniffs at them as it runs. It uses its nose to find food.

A big-eyed owl sits in a nearby tree. The big eyes let in more light and help the owl see even in the dimmest light. The owl can't see the mouse, because the night is too dark. Suddenly, the owl flies straight toward the mouse. The owl can hear so well that it hears even the tiny sound of the mouse running. The mouse squeaks as the owl's claws snatch it up!

The owl and the mouse are only two of the night animals in the meadow. At night a forest or meadow is filled with moths, fireflies, whippoorwills, foxes, raccoons, bats, and other animals. All night long, these night animals hunt and eat in their world of darkness, sounds, and smells.

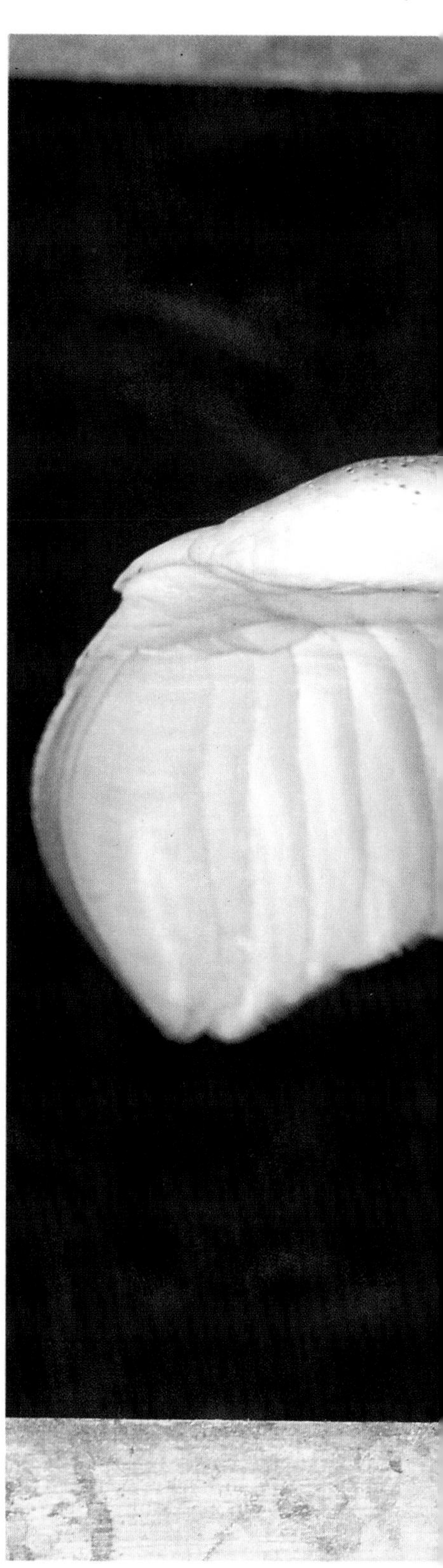

Barn Owl

The owl has caught a mouse and will eat it. Owls and mice are night animals.

Hot and cold

A kangaroo rat's world is the burning hot desert.

The desert is baked by the sun. The air above the sand is so hot it wiggles! During the day, a kangaroo rat sleeps in a cool, underground hole. There it is safe from the terrible heat.

When the sun goes down, the desert cools. Then the rat comes out. It scampers about, looking for seeds that blow across the desert. The rat doesn't look for water. Even if there were water, the kangaroo rat wouldn't drink it. The kangaroo rat never drinks! Its body is able to make the water it needs out of just the dry seeds the rat eats.

Kangaroo rats live in deserts. These rats never drink water. They stay in their cool, underground homes during the hot day.

Kangaroo Rat

Walruses

Walruses live where it's always cold and icy. But a walrus is kept warm by the thick fat under its skin.

A walrus lives in a world of cold water and floating islands of ice.

A walrus swims to the edge of an ice island and sticks his two, long front teeth, called tusks, into the ice. He pulls himself right out of the water with his tusks. Then he lies on the ice in the sunshine, just as you would lie on a sandy beach. Thick, tough skin with lots of thick fat underneath helps keep the walrus warm.

Differences in each animal's body help it stay alive in its world. A kangaroo rat has what it needs to stay alive in a hot desert. A walrus has what it needs to stay alive in its cold, icy world. A kangaroo rat and a walrus could never change places with each other.

Trunks and tails

Wouldn't it seem strange to have a hand on the end of your nose? But an elephant has a sort of hand on the end of its nose.

The elephant's trunk is its nose. And at the end of the trunk are one or two little bumps that the elephant can use as fingers. An elephant can reach up with its trunk and tear leaves from a tree. Then the elephant curls its trunk down and stuffs the leaves into its mouth. An ele-

African Elephant

An elephant uses the tip of its trunk like a hand.

Howler Monkey

This monkey can use its tail as an extra arm.

phant can pick up a tiny peanut with its trunk. And an elephant can use its trunk like a club, to hit a tiger and knock it head over heels!

Woolly monkeys, howler monkeys, and some other kinds of South American monkeys have tails that are nearly as handy as an elephant's trunk. These monkeys use their tails to catch hold of branches as the monkeys swing through the trees. One of these monkeys can hang by its tail from a branch and pull fruit from another branch with its hands. Having that kind of tail is just like having an extra arm!

Curiosities

Platypus

The platypus, or duckbill, is a mammal, but it seems to be part bird, too. It has a body like a beaver and a bill and feet like a duck. A mother platypus gives milk, as all mammal mothers do. But she also lays eggs, as all bird mothers do!

Echidna

The echidna is a mammal, but it's mixed-up just like the platypus. A mother echidna gives milk, as mammal mothers do. But she also lays eggs, like a bird. The echidna is also called a spiny anteater. It eats ants and termites.

Curiosities

Ajolote

The strange lizard called an ajolote looks like a worm with two legs! It uses its two tiny legs to help it crawl and to dig underground holes where it hides during the day. Ajolotes are found only in Lower California.

Glass Snake

The glass snake isn't made of glass. It isn't even a snake. It's a lizard—without legs. You can tell it isn't a snake because it has eyelids. No real snake has eyelids. If you picked up a glass snake by the tail, its tail would break off! Many lizards have tails that break off and grow again. But snakes don't.

Curiosities

Walking Fish

This fish will drown if it stays underwater too long! It has to come to the top of the water once in a while to gulp air. Sometimes it even crawls out of the water! It walks on land, pulling itself along with its fins.

Giant Squid

The giant squid is so big that people once thought it was a sea monster! From the tail to the tip of the long arms, it measures up to 55 feet (17 m). That's fifty-five times as long as its picture on this page. The eye of a giant squid is about as wide as this open book.

The biggest and the smallest

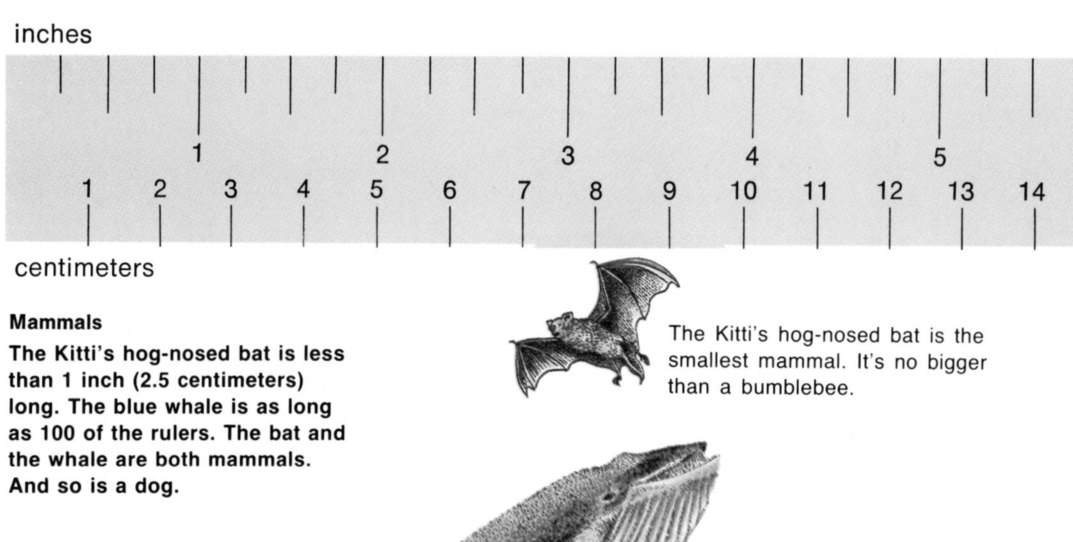

Mammals

The Kitti's hog-nosed bat is less than 1 inch (2.5 centimeters) long. The blue whale is as long as 100 of the rulers. The bat and the whale are both mammals. And so is a dog.

The Kitti's hog-nosed bat is the smallest mammal. It's no bigger than a bumblebee.

The blue whale is the biggest mammal. It's as long as five elephants in a row.

Birds

The bee hummingbird is 2 inches (5 centimeters) long. The ostrich is as tall as eight of the rulers. The hummingbird and the ostrich are both birds. And so is a sparrow.

The ostrich is the biggest bird. It's taller than a tall person.

The bee hummingbird is the smallest bird. It's no longer than one of your fingers.

Reptiles

The West Indian gecko is 2 inches (5 centimeters) long. The reticulate python is as long as 30 of the rulers. The gecko and the python are both reptiles. So is a turtle.

The West Indian gecko is the smallest reptile. It can lie in a teaspoon.

The reticulate python is one of the longest reptiles. It is as long as six bicycles in a row.

Amphibians

The Cuban arrow-poison frog is about ½ inch (1 centimeter) long. The giant salamander is as long as five of the rulers. The salamander and frog are both amphibians. So is a toad.

The Cuban arrow-poison frog is the smallest amphibian. It's about the size of a small coin.

The giant salamander is the biggest amphibian. It's about as long as a bicycle.

Fish

The dwarf pygmy goby is about ½ inch (1 centimeter) long. The whale shark is as long as 50 of the rulers. The goby and the whale shark are both fish. So is a goldfish.

The dwarf pygmy goby is the smallest fish. It's no longer than your fingernail.

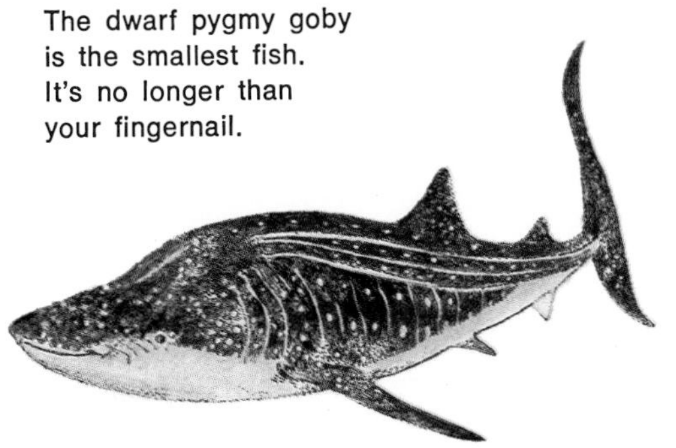

The whale shark is the biggest fish. It's a little longer than a railroad train boxcar.

Arthropods

A mite is smaller than a dot. A giant spider crab is as wide as 13 of the rulers. The mite and the spider crab are both arthropods. And so is an ant.

A mite is the smallest arthropod. The smallest mites are so tiny you can't see them without a microscope.

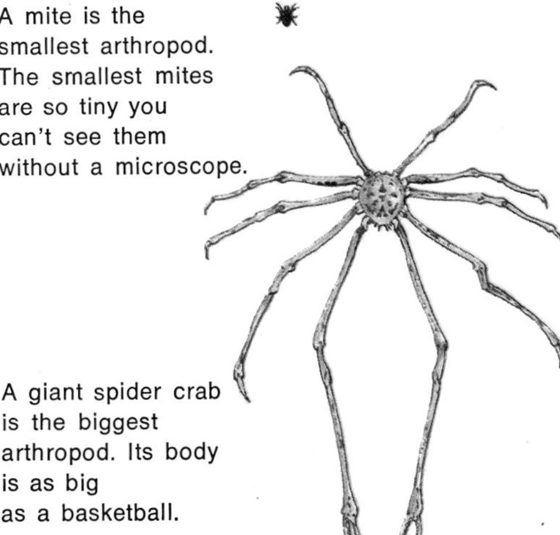

A giant spider crab is the biggest arthropod. Its body is as big as a basketball.

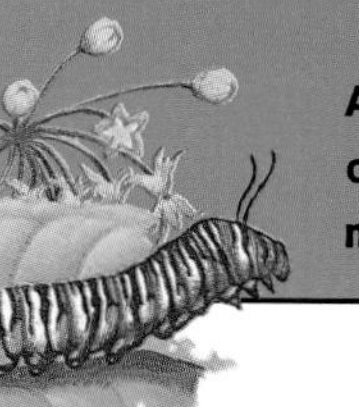

A monarch butterfly caterpillar can live wherever there are milkweed plants.

Living Together

Everywhere in the world, different kinds of plants and animals live together.

Some animals eat plants they live with. Some animals eat other animals they live with. Some animals move far in search of food. Some animals stay near the same place. But all these animals and plants are important to each other—and to us!

If it weren't for some insects, many kinds of plants could not have seeds. If many plant-eating animals didn't have natural enemies that eat them, the plants would be destroyed. If there were no worms and other tiny creatures that live underground there would be no rich soil for the roots of plants. And if there were no green plants, there would be no animals —and no people.

It takes all the plants and animals living together to keep the earth a good place for them—and us—to live in.

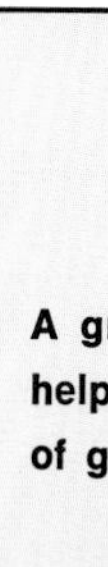

A grasshopper mouse helps keep the number of grasshoppers down.

A wolverine is the natural enemy of many animals.

A giant panda lives only where bamboo plants grow.

Plants and animals need each other

Plants and animals trade with each other. They trade for things they both need to stay alive.

Animals breathe air. The air gets changed inside their bodies. When they breathe the air out again there's something called carbon in it. Animals can't use this air again. But plants need carbon. They take the carbon out of the air—and then animals can breathe the air again. The plants trade fresh air for the carbon they need.

Plants make food from carbon and water. They use sunlight for this work, just as a machine uses gasoline or electricity to keep running. The plants store the food they make inside themselves. Many animals eat plants and then the animals' bodies store up the food that was in the plants. Other animals, such as foxes, wolves, and lions, eat animals that eat plants and get the plant food that's stored in the animals' bodies. So plants are really feeding all animals.

But what do the plants get in return? Many things. Plants make food from the carbon and other things that come from animals' bodies. The animals we call insects carry pollen from one flower to another and the pollen forms seeds. Birds and other animals eat the fruit in which seeds grow and often drop the seeds where they can sprout into new plants. So animals help make new plants grow.

Plants and animals need each other. They couldn't stay alive without each other.

Bumblebee

As a bee gets food from a flower, yellow dust called pollen falls on its body. The pollen rubs off on other flowers the bee goes to, and makes new seeds grow.

Why animals live where they do

You eat bacon and cereal for breakfast. A bear eats fish and berries. Some kinds of animals eat only food from plants. Some kinds eat only other animals. Some animals eat both kinds of food. But each kind of animal has its favorite food and must live where it can get what it needs.

Cows eat grass. Zebras and gazelles do, too. So they do not live in the forest, but on big plains where there is plenty of grass to eat. Lions eat gazelles and zebras. So lions live on the big plains, too, where they will be near their kind of food.

Giant pandas live in the mountains in southern China. The pandas eat young bamboo plants. The kind of

bamboo the pandas eat grows only in the mountains where the pandas live. The pandas couldn't move to another part of China. There would be no food for them in another place.

Koalas live in Australia. They eat only the leaves of 12 kinds of eucalyptus trees. And the koalas can eat only a few of the leaves on each tree. So a koala must live where there are plenty of eucalyptus trees.

Meat-eating animals must live near the animals they eat. Plant-eating animals must live near the plants they eat. And each kind of plant must live in the place that's just right for it. That's why, everywhere in the world, some kinds of plants and animals always live together.

Cheetahs, Zebras, and Giraffes

Plant-eaters, such as zebras and giraffes, live where the plants they eat grow. Meat-eaters, such as cheetahs, live where the plant-eaters do.

Nature's clean-up crew

What becomes of the leaves that fall in the forest every autumn? What keeps them from piling up each year and covering the world with leaves?

Each spring, millions of baby insects eat into the leaves that lie on the ground. Mold grows inside the leaves, making them rot. The leaves begin to fall apart.

Earthworms, insects called springtails, and tiny spiderlike mites go to work. They chew and grind the leaves into pieces. The leaves are digested and pass out of their bodies and into the ground as waste. Mold and very tiny creatures called bacteria change the waste into gas and liquid. And by next fall, nothing is left of most of last year's leaves.

The insects, earthworms, mold, and bacteria are nature's clean-up crew. They're mighty important to us, for without them the world would be a big garbage dump! They help get rid of every dead thing from autumn leaves to elephants.

But the clean-up crew does even more than just get rid of garbage. The clean-up crew turns all dead plants and animals into things that plants can use. The gas and liquid that dead, rotting things become is needed by plants. Without it they couldn't grow or live. And without plants there could be no animals or people.

Without the crawling animals and the mold and bacteria of the clean-up crew—we couldn't live!

Slugs and baby insects live in fallen leaves. Below the leaves live mites and springtails, shown in circles. Worms and mole crickets live farther down.

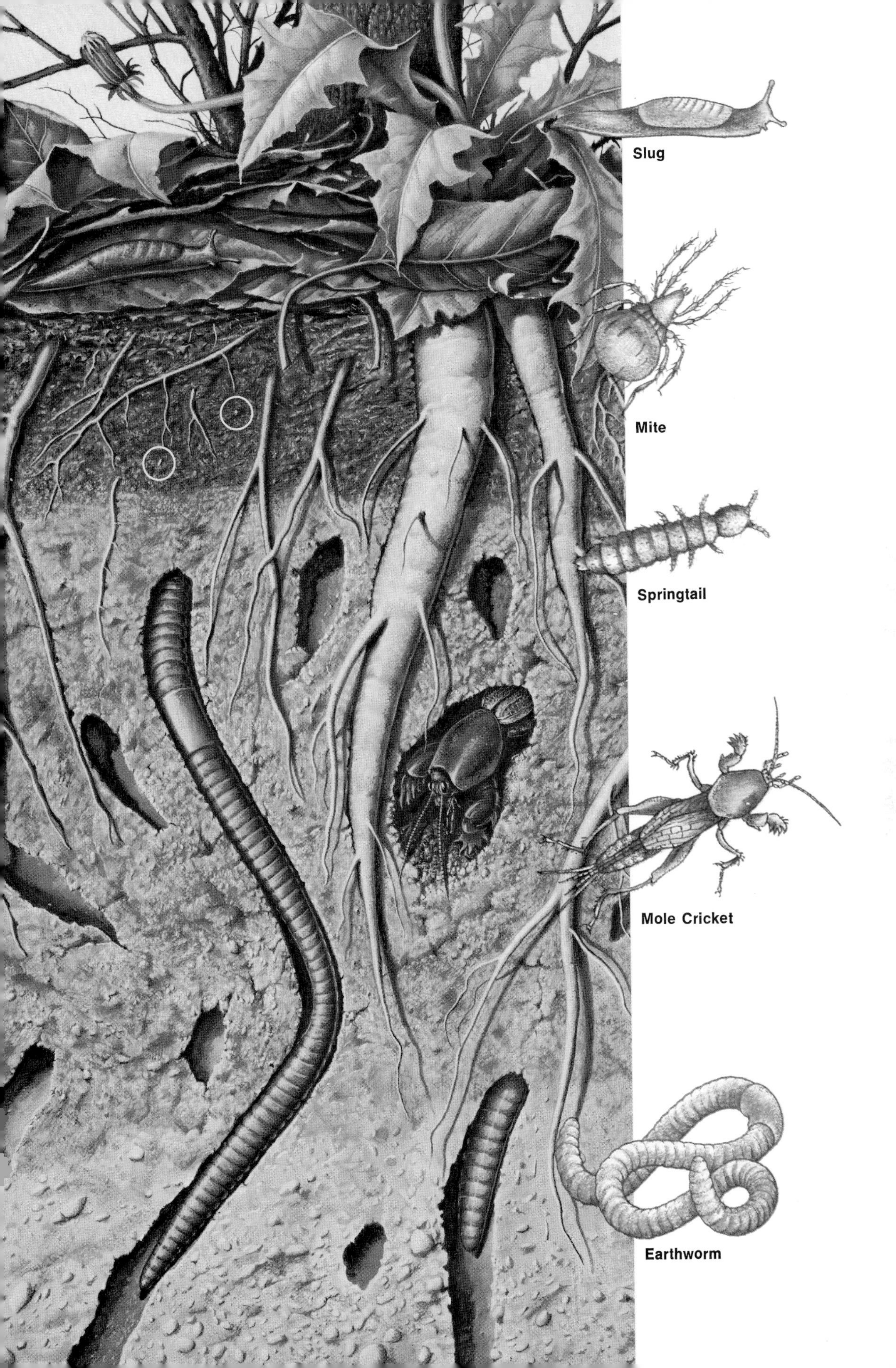

Slug
Mite
Springtail
Mole Cricket
Earthworm

Life in low places and high places

Underground caves are blacker than a lump of coal. Mountaintops are cold and bare. It doesn't seem possible for animals to live in these places. But animals do live in them.

Small, white fish swim in a stream in an underground cave. The fish have no eyes! There is no light at all in the cave, so eyes would be of no use to the fish.

But even though they are blind, the fish never bump into anything or each other. These fish can feel things in the water before they touch them.

One of the fish swims toward the side of the cave. A tiny, eyeless, pale crayfish is hanging from a rock. The

Rocky Mountain Goat and Kid

Mountain goats can climb to the highest, narrowest parts of a mountain. Their hoofs keep them from slipping.

fish rushes forward and gulps down the crayfish. The fish can feel and smell so well that it can find food easily.

On a mountaintop far, far above the cave, a Rocky Mountain goat is looking for plants to eat. The goat climbs higher and higher. The way is steep and narrow, but the goat climbs easily. Its cuplike hoofs keep it from slipping. The goat can go where no other animal can follow. The goat is right at home on the high, steep mountaintop.

Millions of years ago animals moved into every place in the world where they could go. That's why today there are animals living in even the highest and lowest places. And the animals all changed to fit the places where they lived. That's why Rocky Mountain goats don't slip and cave fish don't need eyes.

The cave fish has no eyes. It doesn't need them in its coal-black world. It finds its food by feel and smell.

Cave Fish

Keep out!

Some animals hunt for food in many different places and sleep wherever they happen to be. But other animals always sleep and hunt in the same place. This place is their territory.

A dragonfly's territory is a space about as big as a room. An owl's territory may be a meadow or part of a woods. An ape family's territory is usually several hundred trees in a jungle. Even some kinds of fish have territories in which they swim about and never leave.

Most animals guard their territories. Some of them even put "Keep Out" signs on the edges of their territories. Deer, bears, and many other animals rub against trees and leave a smell that says "Keep Out" to others. A wolverine puts a "Keep Off" smell on any food it finds, but doesn't eat, in its territory. The songs of many birds are a way of saying "Keep out of my territory" to other birds.

If too many of the same kind of animals lived in one territory, there might not be enough food for all. So most animals try to keep animals like themselves out of their territory. Some animals won't even let their own young stay in the territory after they grow up.

Animals don't seem to mind if different kinds of animals share their territory. But if an animal like themselves tries to move in—they will fight to keep it out.

Mockingbirds defend their territory. So when this owl came into its territory, the mockingbird attacked.

With a hard peck the mockingbird lets the surprised owl know that it better keep out of mockingbird territory.

Mockingbird and Great Horned Owl

Keeping things even

Once, several thousand deer and a few dozen mountain lions lived together in a part of Arizona. Each year, the mountain lions ate hundreds of deer. But, during the year, hundreds of new deer were born. So there was always just about the same number of deer. And there was always just about the same number of mountain lions.

There weren't too many mountain lions, so they always had plenty to eat. There weren't too many deer, so the deer had plenty to eat. Everything was even.

Then, the mountain lions killed some farm animals. The farmers began to hunt the mountain lions. Soon, the mountain lions there had all been killed.

After that, baby deer that would have been killed by mountain lions were able to grow up. Many of them had babies. Soon, there were many more deer than there had been when the mountain lions were eating them. Things weren't even any more.

Now there were so many deer that there wasn't enough food for all of them.

In the summer, they ate up most of the food that would have kept them alive during the winter.

And when winter came, thousands of the deer starved to death.

Animals keep things even by living together. As long as things are even, the animals are all right. But sometimes men change things so they're no longer even, and then there is trouble for the animals—and often for people, too.

Mule Deer

Natural enemies

Most animals have natural enemies—other animals that like to eat them.

It's night on a desert in the United States. A wolf spider is hunting. The spider is the natural enemy of beetles and other insects.

The spider, hurrying over the sand, meets a scorpion. And the scorpion is the spider's natural enemy. With its two front claws the scorpion grabs the spider. The scorpion's long tail flashes down and its sharp sting stabs into the spider. Then the scorpion begins to eat the spider.

After a while the scorpion finishes. A bright-eyed grasshopper mouse comes around a rock. The mouse sees the scorpion. The mouse dashes forward and bites off the scorpion's poisonous tail. Then the mouse pushes the scorpion into its mouth. This kind of mouse is the natural enemy of the scorpion.

The mouse cleans its whiskers and trots off. Suddenly, something swoops through the air. It's a screech owl—the mouse's natural enemy. The owl grabs the mouse with its sharp claws.

Few other animals hunt owls to eat, so the owl is safe from natural enemies. So are wolves, bears, lions, tigers, and other big meat-eating animals. Old age is their worst enemy. For when a hunting animal gets too old to move quickly, it can't catch anything. Then it starves to death.

Scorpion and Spider

The yellow scorpion has caught the brown spider and will eat it. A scorpion is a spider's natural enemy.

Eohippus

Scientists think the eohippus was the ancestor of the modern horse. The eohippus was a small animal that had toes instead of hoofs.

Change or die!

Suppose that all the milkweed plants in the world suddenly died. What would happen to monarch butterfly caterpillars? They eat only milkweed leaves.

The mother monarch butterflies would have to lay their eggs on another kind of plant. And the caterpillars would have to learn to eat the leaves of that plant. Otherwise the caterpillars would die, and soon there would be no monarch butterflies.

If the monarch butterflies changed, and learned to eat another kind of plant, we would say they had adapted. And if they didn't change, and all died, we would say they were extinct.

Millions of years ago giant reptiles called dinosaurs were everywhere. Maybe the world got too cold for them. Maybe something happened to their food. But

American Saddle Horse

The American saddle horse is a favorite of people who like to ride horses. The adult horse is 4.8 to 5.4 feet (1.44 to 1.62 meters) high at the withers (shoulders).

whatever happened, the dinosaurs weren't able to adapt. There are no dinosaurs alive today. They are all extinct.

Millions of years ago there were tiny horses with toes instead of hoofs. They lived in forests and ate leaves. Then something happened. Maybe there wasn't enough food. Maybe the forests became too dangerous. But the horses learned to live on the plains and eat grass. They adapted.

The horses of today came from those long-ago horses that adapted. In fact, every kind of animal in the world today came from animals that adapted long, long ago.

The Pteranodon was a flying reptile.

Animals of Long Ago

Imagine animals like fish with legs. Imagine trees like giant feather dusters. That's what some animals and trees looked like, once.

Just as you change as you grow older, the world changes and the things that live on it change. Most scientists believe that the world has changed many times in the past. And many kinds of animals have lived on it.

Once there were scaly reptiles as big as houses. Once there were horses no bigger than cats. And once, very long ago, there were no animals of any kind living on the land. All the animals lived in water.

The next few pages will show you some of the strange animals that once lived on the earth.

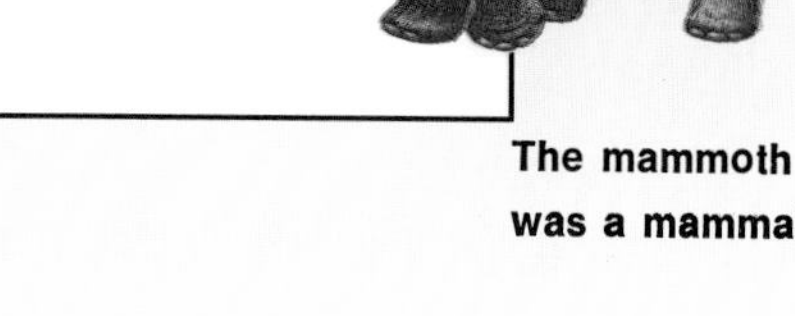

The mammoth was a mammal.

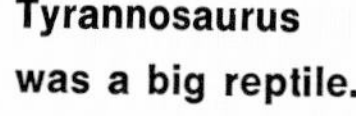

Tyrannosaurus was a big reptile.

Triceratops
was a reptile.

Strange sea animals

Scientists say that five hundred million years ago all plants and animals lived in the sea. There were sponges, jellyfish, worms with legs, and things like clams.

And there was another animal that moved busily everywhere over the rocks and sand. It had big, buglike eyes and feelers and many legs. It looked like a crab and insect mixed together. This animal was a trilobite.

Some trilobites were as big as your fist. Most were no bigger than a quarter. They were no smarter than insects. But 500 million years ago, trilobites were the biggest and smartest animals in the whole world.

Use this small picture to find out the names of the animals in the big picture.

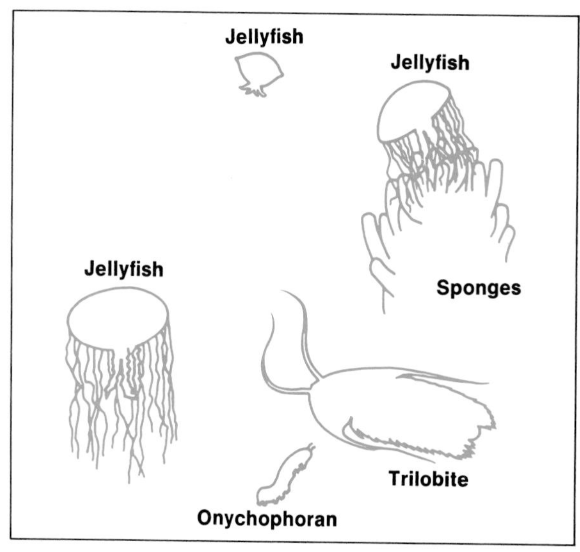

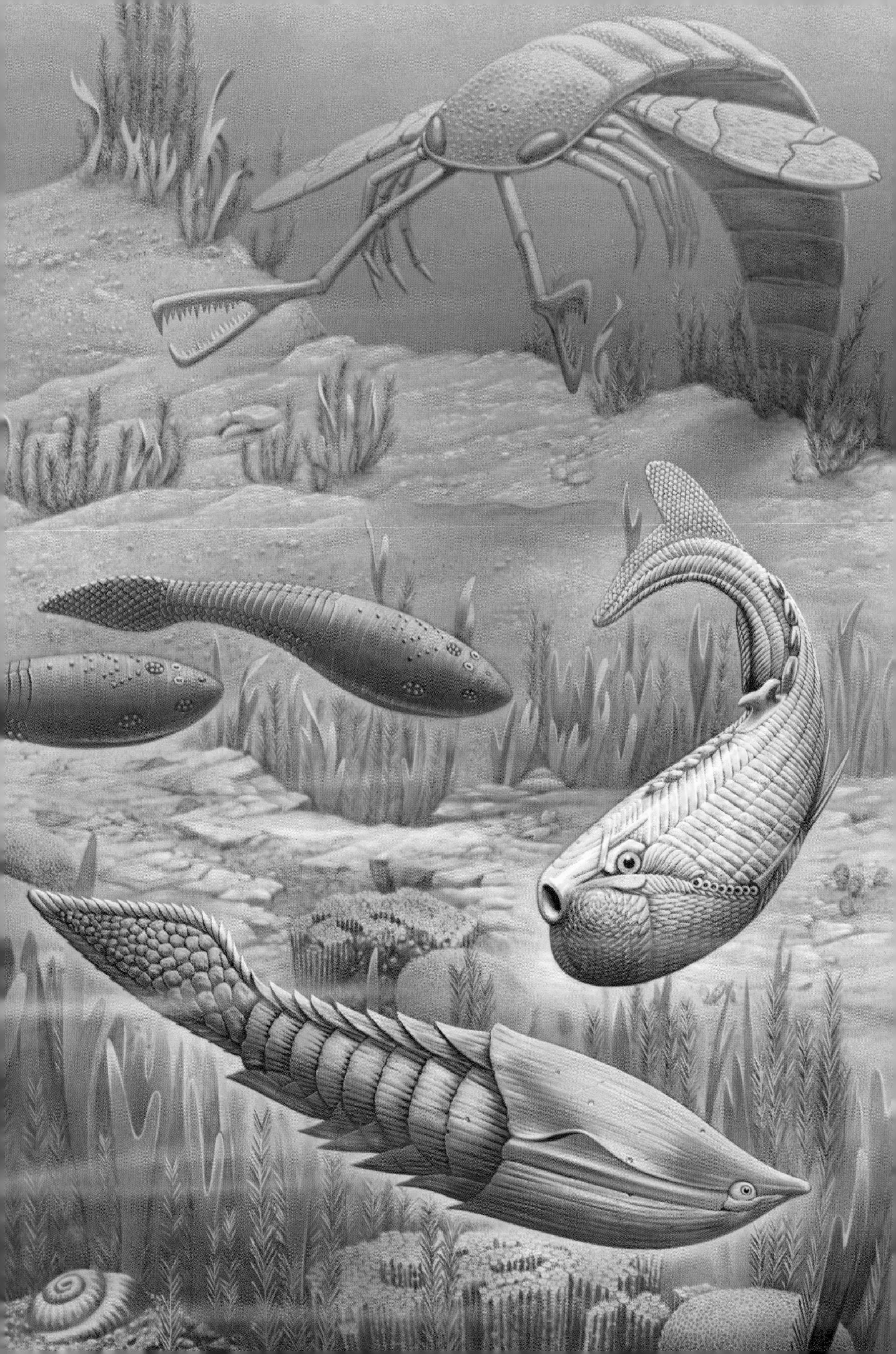

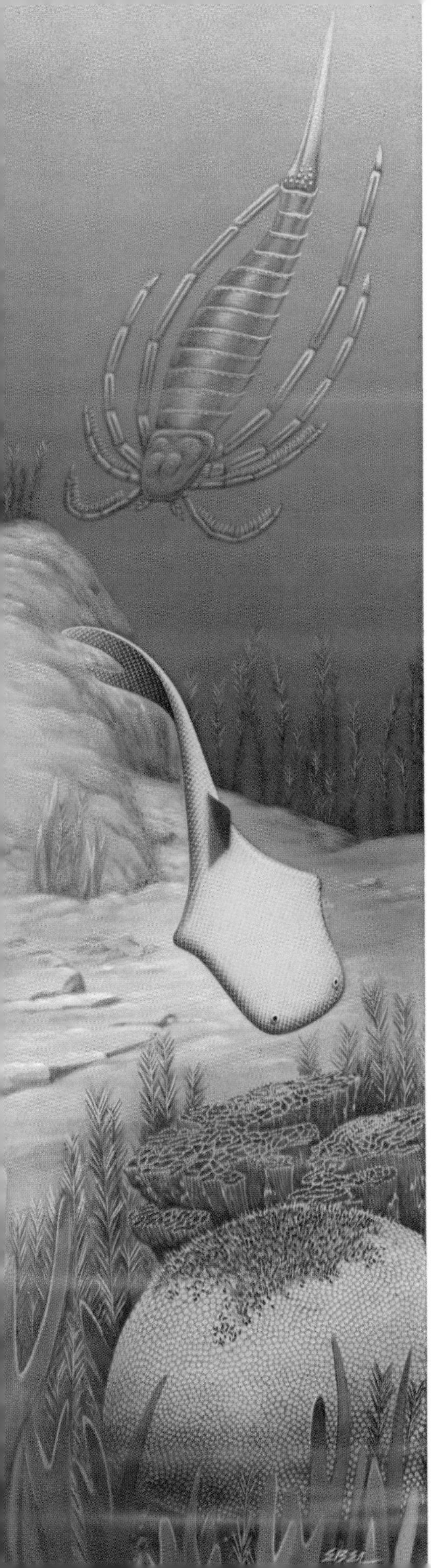

Fish in armor

According to most scientists, the fishes that swam in the seas 430 million years ago were covered with hard, bony armor. They had no jaws like the fish of today. Their mouths were just holes in the bony shells that covered their heads. They sucked food through the holes as they swam slowly over the sea-bottom.

The armored fish weren't the only animals in the water. There were creatures with many legs, like insects. They were big and fast and they ate other animals. The armored fish were smaller and slower. They needed their armor for protection.

Use this small picture
to find out the names of the
animals in the big picture.

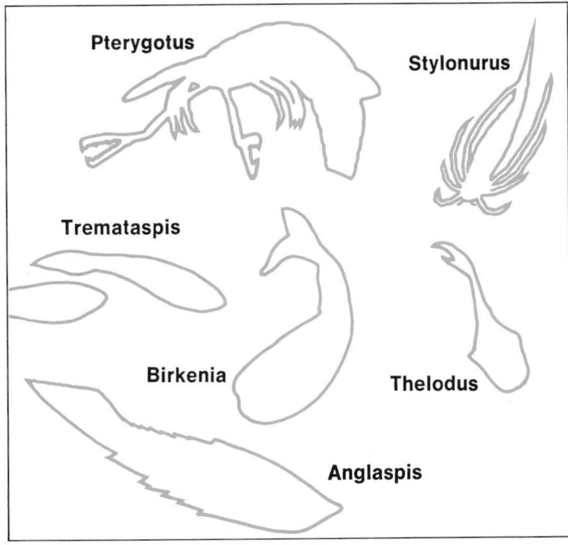

The first four-footed animal

Imagine a fish with legs!

Once upon a time, there really was an animal that looked like a fish with legs. Most scientists believe that about 400 million years ago it swam in the warm, green waters of swamps and lagoons. It also walked about on the muddy shore.

This creature was probably the first four-footed animal in the world. It was also one of the very first amphibians—the great, great granddaddy of today's frogs, toads, and salamanders.

Use this small picture to find out the names of the animals in the big picture.

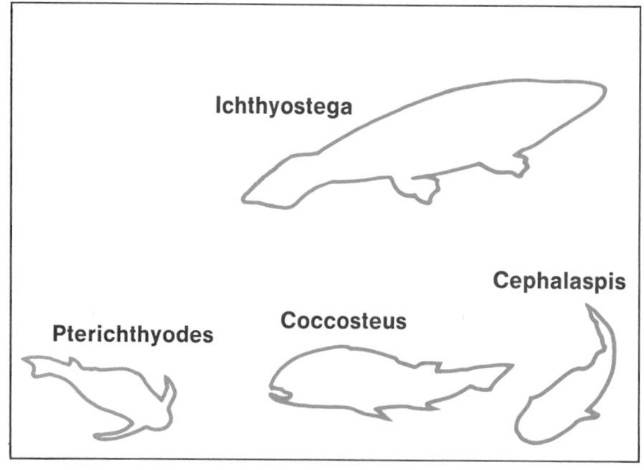

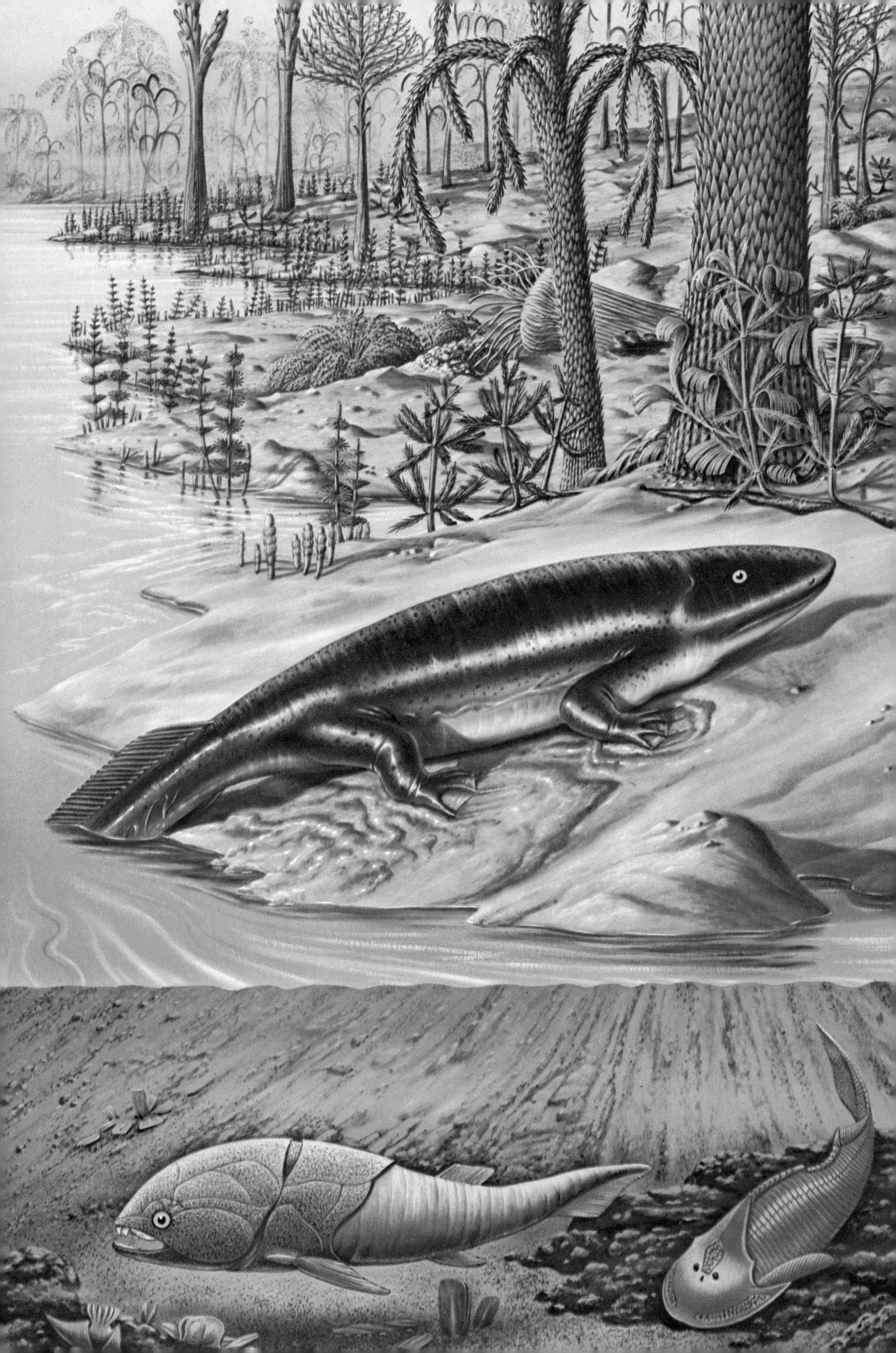

A 250-million-year-old puzzle

Scientists tell us that about 250 million years ago there lived a big reptile called Dimetrodon. It was about as long as a small automobile. It ate smaller reptiles.

Dimetrodon had a big fin like a sail on its back. Scientists think the fin helped a Dimetrodon warm up

or cool off. After a cool night, a stiff, cold Dimetrodon might lie with its fin facing the sun, and the fin would quickly get warm. The warmth would spread into the Dimetrodon's body. But a Dimetrodon that was too hot could lie with the thin edge of the fin facing the sun. Then, the fin would cool off.

Dimetrodon

Coelophysis

Turtles and terrible lizards

According to most scientists, the first dinosaurs came into the world about 225 million years ago. And along with them came the first turtles.

The word *dinosaur* means *terrible lizard.* But the first dinosaurs weren't very terrible. Some were no bigger than chickens. The biggest were not much taller than a tall man. It wasn't until millions of years later that there were giant dinosaurs.

The first turtles looked much like turtles do now. Turtles' shapes must be just right for them. They haven't changed much in 225 million years.

Triassochelys

The biggest dinosaurs

You could have walked beneath an Apatosaurus and your head wouldn't even have touched its stomach.

An Apatosaurus was as long as four big elephants standing in a line. The word *Apatosaurus* means "untrue lizard." The man who named it thought such a huge creature could not have been real. Apatosaurus is also sometimes called Brontosaurus, which means "thunder lizard."

The dinosaur called Brachiosaurus was even bigger. It was as long as five big elephants standing in a line. And it was so tall that it could have looked over the top of a four-story building.

Scientists say that these two kinds of dinosaurs lived about 150 million years ago. They were big, but not dangerous to other animals, for they ate only plants.

Brachiosaurus

Apatosaurus

Flying reptiles

No reptile that lives today—snake, turtle, lizard, alligator, or crocodile—can fly. And no reptile of today has hair on its body. But scientists say that 150 million years ago there were many flying reptiles. And some scientists think that some of the reptiles may have had a kind of hair on their bodies.

Most of the flying reptiles of 150 million years ago were about the size of bats of today. And the reptiles probably flew much as bats do.

The flying reptiles flapped and fluttered and glided over lakes and seashores and grabbed up fish in their long jaws. They probably climbed trees and hung head down from branches, with their wings folded around themselves like blankets.

Rhamphorhynchus

The first birds

The birds of today sing or whistle or screech. But the first birds may have hissed like snakes! They were more like reptiles than like birds. They were reptiles with wings and feathers.

The first birds we know about were as big as pigeons. They had little claws on their wings and teeth in their mouths. They probably couldn't fly very well, but they could climb trees easily. Most scientists believe that the first birds lived about 150 million years ago, at the same time as some of the big dinosaurs.

Tyrannosaurus the meat-eater

One of the most fierce-looking dinosaurs was Tyrannosaurus. Scientists can tell from its sharp teeth that it was a meat-eater. But they're not sure how it got its food.

Some scientists think Tyrannosaurus was a fierce hunter. They think it chased other dinosaurs, attacked them, and killed them for food!

But other scientists think Tyrannosaurus must have been too big and heavy to run fast. They think it just waddled around, looking for the bodies of dead dinosaurs, and ate them.

What do you think?

Tyrannosaurus

Stories in stone

There were no people on the world when dinosaurs were alive. So how do we know about dinosaurs and other animals of long ago?

Sometimes, when a dinosaur died, its body lay on muddy ground. The soft parts rotted away, but mud covered the bones and kept them from rotting.

Bones are full of tiny holes. Water, trickling through the mud, seeped into the dinosaur bones. Rock that was dissolved in the water, filled the many holes. In time, the bones were filled with rock. This helped preserve them.

Over millions of years, the mud covering the bones turned into rock. Over many more millions of years, sun and rain wore away the rock, revealing the rocky skeleton.

Scientists look for rocky skeletons such as this and dig them out of the ground. From such a skeleton the scientists can tell what the animal looked like. They can tell what it ate by the shape of its teeth. They can often even tell how well the animal could see and hear and smell things.

Rocky skeletons and bones are called fossils. There are other kinds of fossils, too. Dinosaurs made footprints in mud and the mud turned to stone with the footprints still in it. Insects were caught in gobs of tree sap that turned into a glasslike stone called amber. Fossils such as these are stories in stone that tell us what the animals of long ago were like.

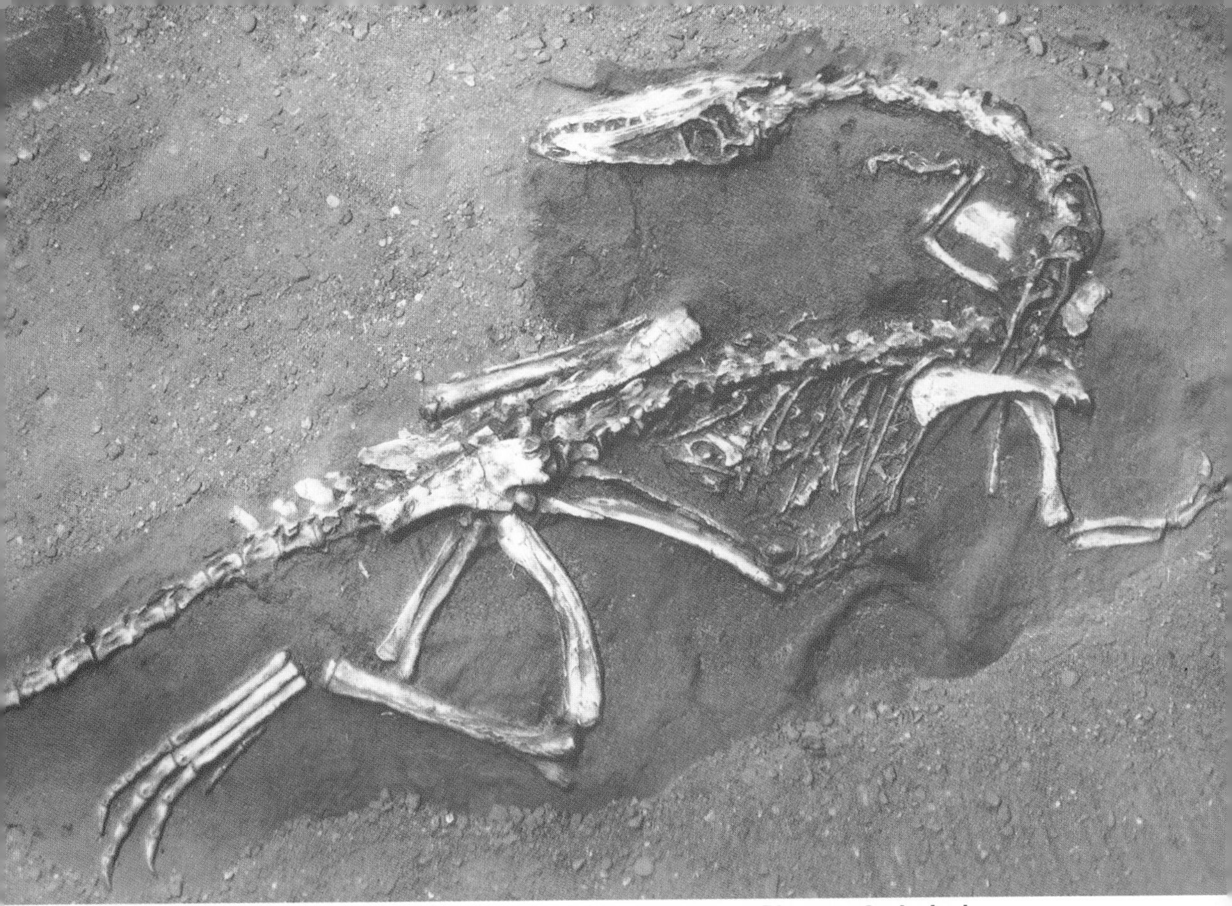

Fossil Skeleton of Dinosaur Coelophysis

These are fossils of animals that died and were covered by mud hundreds of millions of years ago. We can tell what the animals looked like from these fossils.

Fossil Trilobites and Brachiopods

Horses without hoofs

Scientists say that if you could see the horses that lived 55 million years ago, you wouldn't know they were horses. They had toes on their feet instead of hoofs. They ate fruit and leaves instead of grass. And they were no bigger than a medium-sized dog. The name given to these early horses is Eohippus, which means "dawn horse."

Eohippus

Elephants without trunks

Most scientists believe that 50 million years ago there were elephants living in swamps where Egypt is today. But they didn't look anything like elephants do now. The first elephants didn't have trunks or long tusks. And they were about the size of hogs!

Mammoth

Elephants with fur coats

If you could have been in North America or Europe twenty thousand years ago, you'd have thought you were at the North Pole! Much of the land was covered with a mountain of ice and snow.

Many animals that lived then were just like the animals that live in cold places today. There were bears, elk, and packs of wolves. There were also animals that looked like huge elephants, but they were covered with thick, shaggy fur. These animals are called *mammoths,* a word that means *very big.*

Mammoths and dinosaurs and many other animals of long ago are all gone. As many years passed, some of those animals died off and others changed. And animals are still changing. In a million years the world will be as different as it was a million years ago. Many of today's animals will be gone. There may be many new kinds of animals. The story of life on earth is a story that is always changing.

Wolf

People make pictures of animals for magazines and books.

People and Animals

Some people have jobs working with wild animals! These people work in zoos, parks, animal hospitals, museums, and laboratories. Some even work right in the places where wild animals live.

Zookeepers care for animals in zoos. Some kinds of scientists study animals to learn how they live and act. Veterinarians are animal doctors. Game wardens and rangers care for animals in parks and preserves. And there are artists and photographers who make pictures of animals for books and museums.

There are many kinds of jobs for people who like to work with animals.

People study animals to learn more about them.

People take care of animals in zoos and parks.

Taking care of zoo animals

Many people work in a zoo. People called keepers feed the animals and keep them and their cages clean. Animal doctors, called veterinarians, check the animals to keep them healthy and care for them if they get sick. Zoologists study the animals to learn more about them. The next few pages show some of the things done by people who work at the famous London Zoo, in England.

An animal can have a toothache, too. Zookeepers check the animals' teeth to make sure they're all right.

Alligator

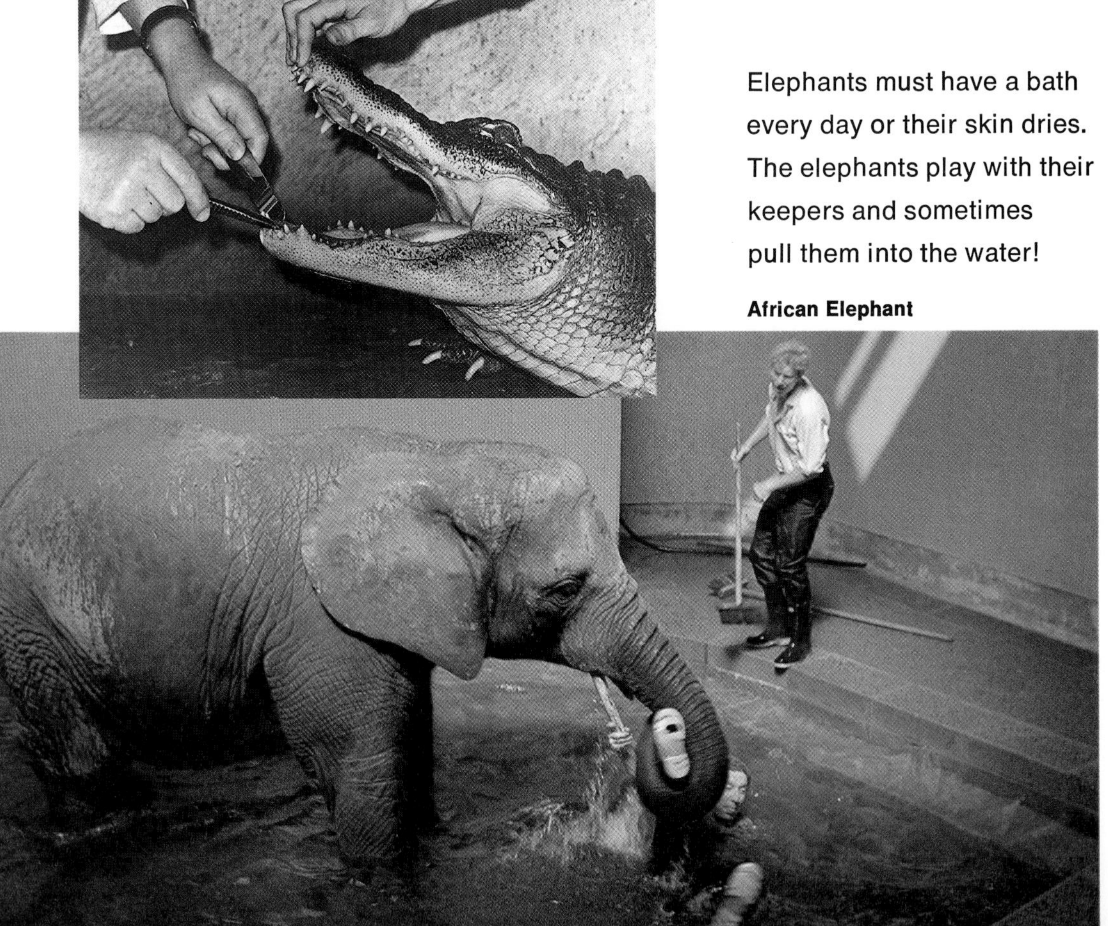

Elephants must have a bath every day or their skin dries. The elephants play with their keepers and sometimes pull them into the water!

African Elephant

Giraffes watch as the zookeeper raises a bunch of leaves up into a tree.

Now the leaves are just high enough for these long-necked animals to eat comfortably.

Giraffes

Rhinoceros

A zookeeper cuts and files a rhinoceros's toenails. If its toenails grow too long, the rhinoceros has trouble walking.

Feeding time

Wild animals can get their own food, but animals in zoos must be fed by keepers. So the keepers have to know what kind of food each animal eats and how much it needs. Feeding the animals is one of the most important parts of taking care of them.

These are dinners for birds. Each tray has chopped fruit, grain, and other things birds like.

A tray of food goes into every bird cage. Each bird gets exactly the right amount of food to keep it healthy.

The zoo must have lots of juicy bamboo plants for the panda every day. That's mainly what a panda eats.

Giant Panda

Lions, tigers, and jaguars don't eat every day in the wild. So they're not fed every day in the zoo, either.

Jaguar

Wild deer never get to eat carrots. But the zookeepers know that carrots are good for a deer.

Red Deer

A children's zoo

A children's zoo is a little zoo inside a big one. The animals in a children's zoo are tame and gentle and can be touched and petted. Many of them are babies, so the keepers in a children's zoo must know how to care for baby animals. The keepers must know a lot about all animals, too, because children who visit the zoo ask lots of questions.

There's a tea party for chimpanzees every afternoon at the London Zoo.

Chimpanzees

Goat

Zookeepers must know a lot about animals. This girl zookeeper is telling children about a goat.

Most animals in a children's zoo are tame and gentle.

Highland Calf

Learning about animals

Biologists, zoologists, and naturalists are scientists who study living things. They often work in laboratories or even in their own homes. But sometimes they go to wild parts of the world to study the animals living there.

The things these scientists learn help us know more about the world around us.

Rhesus Monkey

This zoology student is studying animals in the mountains of India. The rhesus monkey seems to be studying the student.

Canada Geese

This biologist is putting numbered bands on the necks of Canada geese. This will help scientists study the geese after they are turned loose.

Roger Tory Peterson is an artist and photographer who studies birds. He is recording the sounds of king penguins.

King Penguins

Jacques Cousteau has spent his life exploring beneath the ocean. He makes movies of the fish and animals that live in the water.

Jacques Cousteau's crew uses a special camera to take pictures deep in the ocean.

Learning from animals

Some animals are a lot like people. They can be happy or sad or angry. They can be brave or afraid. They can learn things and solve easy problems.

Scientists called psychologists often study these animals to learn why they act as they do. And sometimes this helps the psychologists understand why people act as they do. By studying the animals, psychologists learn more about people.

Dr. Penny Patterson is using a machine to teach Koko, the gorilla, to communicate with people.

Gorilla

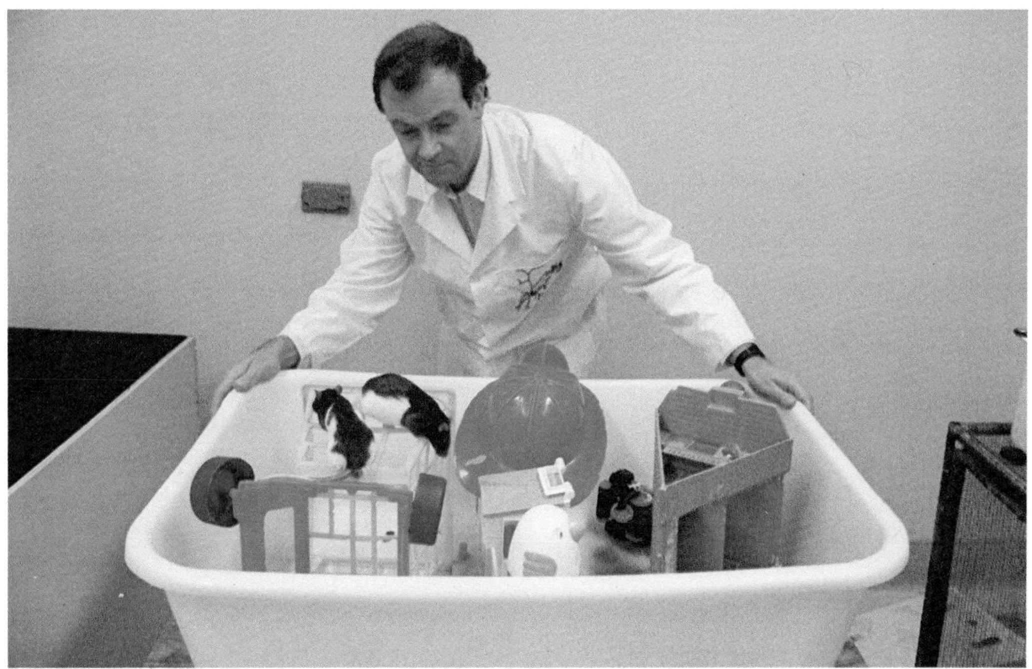

Rats

Dr. William Greenough does experiments with rat behavior at the University of Illinois.

Dr. Konrad Lorenz has spent his life studying animals and making friends with them. He has written many interesting books.

Geese

Taking care of animals

Zookeepers and aquarists, game wardens, and forest rangers are people whose work is to care for animals.

Zookeepers and aquarists are trained to make sure each kind of animal gets the food, care, and medical attention it needs.

Game wardens and rangers help protect the wild animals in national parks and game preserves.

The steenbok was trapped by a flood in Africa. The ranger went to its rescue and brought it to dry land.

Steenbok

Sea Otter

This sea otter was rescued from an oil-polluted shore. The rescue workers are cleaning it.

Alligator

The game warden is going to put a tag on the alligator. Animals are tagged so they can be counted easily.

Getting help from animals

Learning how to make animals well can help scientists learn how to keep people well. Some kinds of animals get the same kinds of diseases people do. By working with animals, scientists and veterinarians have discovered many kinds of medicines and treatments that also help people.

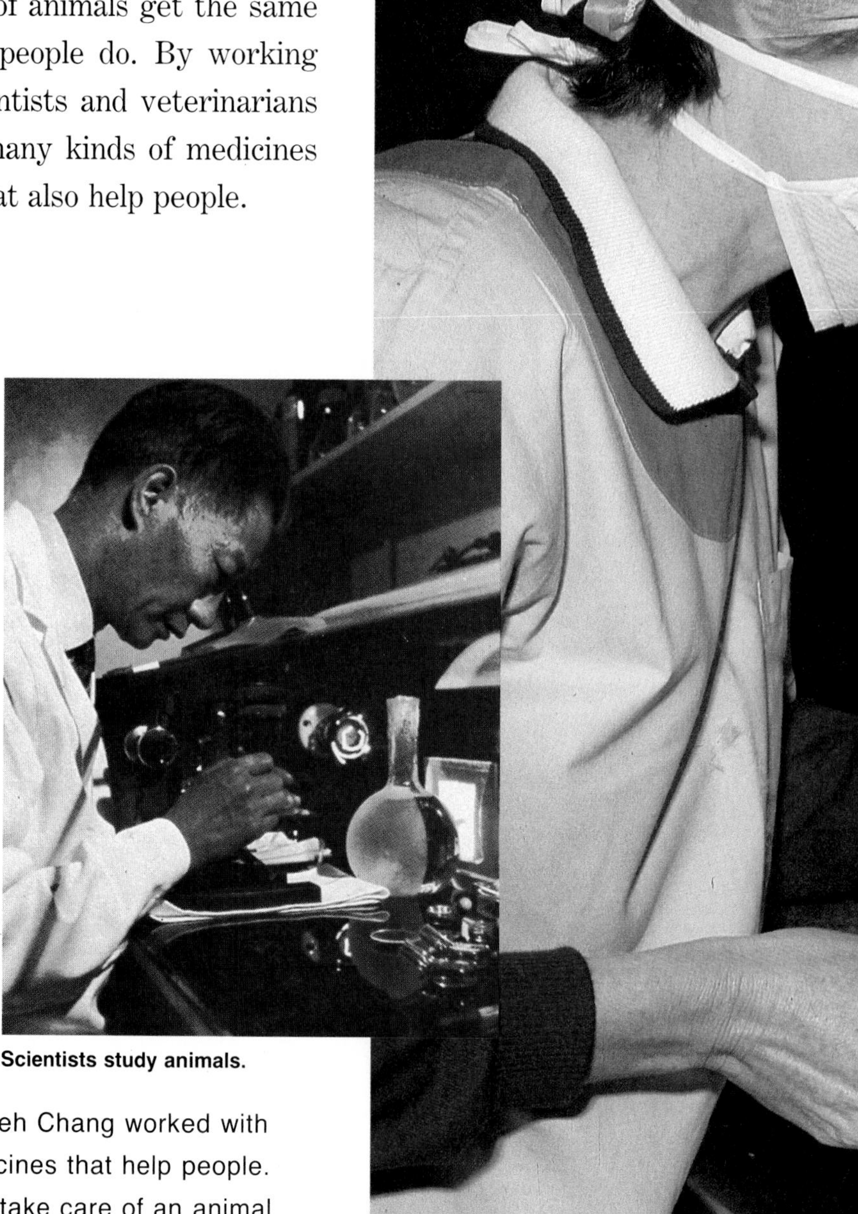

Scientists study animals.

(above) Dr. Min Chueh Chang worked with animals to find medicines that help people. (right) Veterinarians take care of an animal patient.

A veterinarian treats animals.

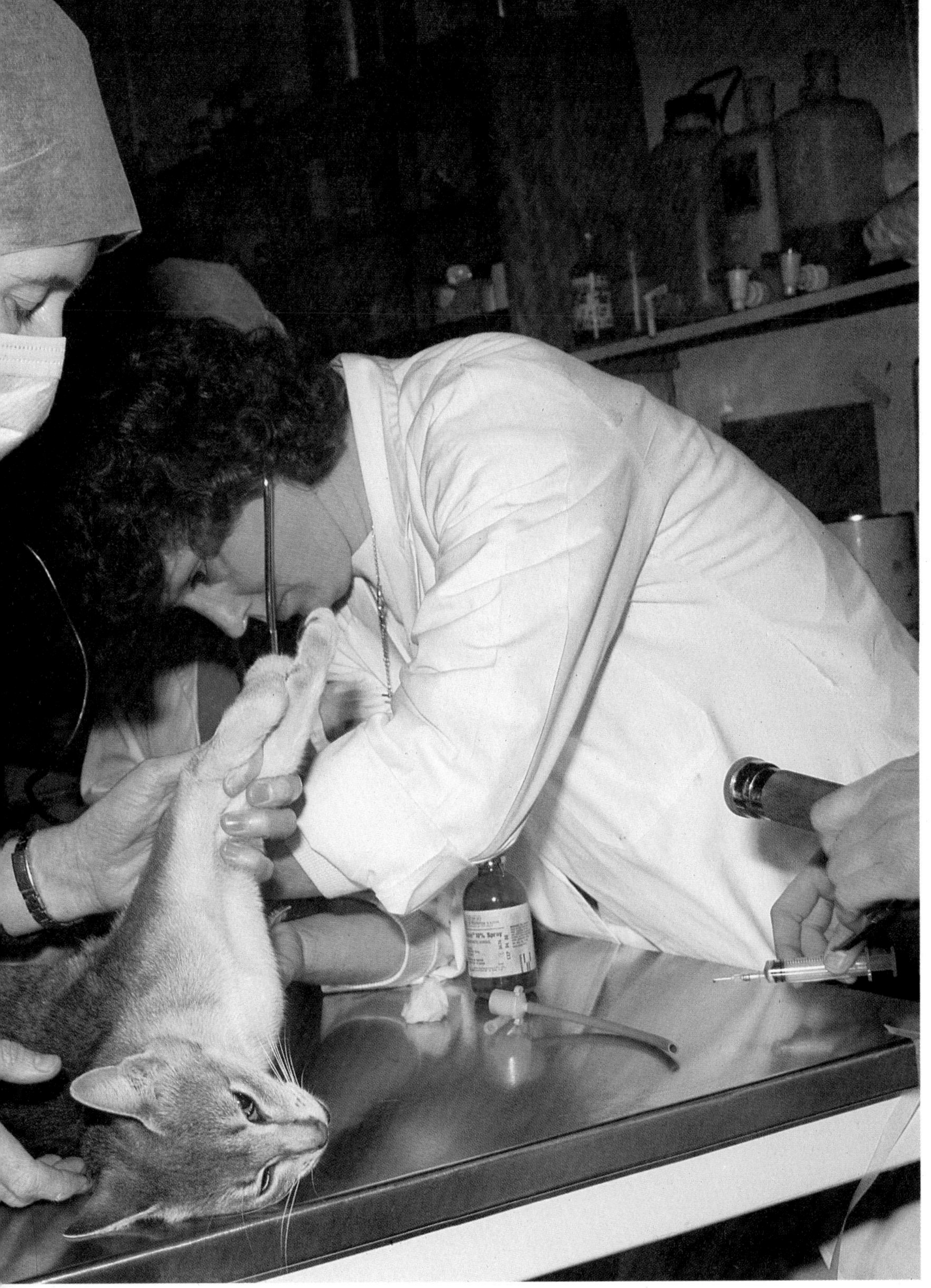

Making pictures of animals

It must be lots of fun to be an animal artist or photographer. These people go everywhere in the world to take and make pictures of different kinds of animals. Their pictures are used in books like this one. They also are used in magazines; by zoos, museums, and libraries; and as decorations in people's homes.

Artist Don Eckelberry spends many hours in the woods looking at the kinds of birds he wants to paint. He makes quick drawings of as many as he sees. Then, with the drawings to help him, he goes back to his studio and begins the painting.

This painting of bobwhites is
by animal artist Don Eckelberry.

The chicken
is a domestic animal.

Domestic Animals

Domestic animals are the animals you see on farms and ranches and in people's homes. Most domestic animals are useful to people in some way.

From some domestic animals we get food—meat, milk, eggs, butter, and cheese.

We get leather and cloth from the skins and hair of some domestic animals.

Some domestic animals do work for people, by carrying heavy loads and pulling carts and wagons.

Some kinds of glue, soap, cooking shortening, and other things are made from the bodies of domestic animals.

Some domestic animals help us have fun. We ride on them or watch them race or do tricks.

And some domestic animals are pets that give us friendship and love.

The Tibetan yak
is a domestic animal.

The Indian elephant
is a domestic animal.

The Angora goat is a domestic animal.

Meat and milk

Cattle are important domestic animals. From beef cattle we get steaks, roast beef, and hamburgers. From dairy cattle we get milk for drinking and for making into cream, butter, cheese, and ice cream.

Most of the leather used for shoes comes from the skin of cattle.

Cattle are raised for milk or meat nearly everywhere in the world.

Milk cows, such as these, are called dairy cattle. Many farms in many parts of the world have small herds of dairy cattle.

Dairy Cattle

Beef Cattle

Steaks, roast beef, and hamburgers come from beef cattle such as these. Beef cattle are usually kept in large herds.

Roast goose is a favorite Christmas dinner in some European countries.

Geese

Chickens and turkeys have white meat and dark meat. But all the meat on a duck is dark.

White Pekin Ducks

Meat and eggs

Do you like scrambled eggs, fried chicken, roast duck? These foods come from birds that are raised on farms. Birds that are raised for food are called poultry. Chickens, ducks, geese, and turkeys are the most important kind of poultry.

Many farms raise some poultry. But some farms raise nothing but poultry. And, of course, these are called poultry farms.

Tom Turkey

Many people have turkey for dinner on Thanksgiving Day in the United States.

Chickens are raised on farms for their eggs and meat.

White Rock Hen

This sheep is ready to be sheared. Its wool coat is thick and heavy.

The wool is carefully sheared off in one piece. This doesn't hurt the sheep.

Sheep

These sheep have had their wool sheared off. The wool will soon begin to grow again.

Meat and cloth

Sheep are important. Clothes, blankets, and many other things are made from their wool.

There are big flocks of sheep on farms in many parts of the world. Once or twice a year, all the sheep have their wool cut off. This is called shearing. The wool is sent to factories where it is made into cloth.

We get food from sheep, too. Leg of lamb, lamb chops, and mutton come from sheep.

French Angora Rabbit

Angora rabbit fur is used to make fine, soft cloth.

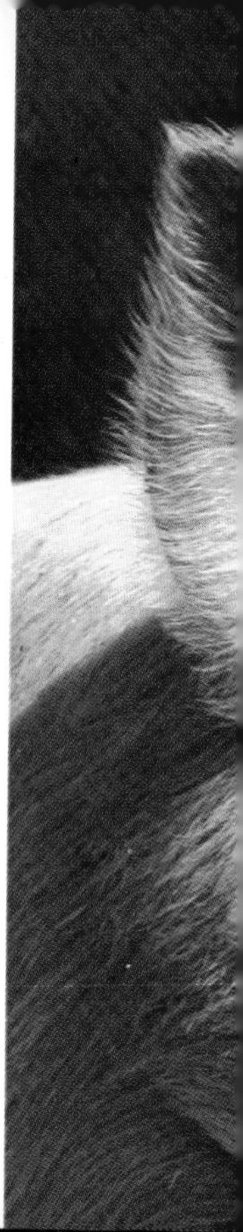

Meat and much more

Someone once said that people can use every part of a hog but its squeal. That's nearly true. From hogs we get ham, bacon, pork chops, roast pork, sausages, spare ribs —even pickled pig's feet. The skin of hogs is made into gloves, shoes, and belts. Hog fat is made into lard, soap, and shaving cream. Hog hair is used in brushes, and ground hog bones are made into glue.

These hogs won a prize in a contest. One reason they won was that they have lots of meat and not much fat.

Prize Hogs

Hogs give us meat, bacon, fat, and many other products.

Yorkshire Hog

An adult female hog is a sow. A baby hog, less than ten weeks old, is called a pig or piglet.

Sow and Pigs

Thoroughbred Horse

Thoroughbreds are slim, handsome horses that can run fast. They are raised for riding and jumping.

Work and play

Horses have been useful to people for thousands of years. People used to do much of their traveling by riding on horses or in carriages that horses pulled. Horses pulled plows and wagons on farms.

Today, machines do most of the work that horses once did. But horses are still raised for riding, racing, and other sports. And in some parts of the world, horses still do a lot of work, too.

In Turkestan, horses are trained for a game called Buzkashi. They must be able to stop, turn, and kneel, quickly.

Bactrian Stallions

Big, strong horses are raised to pull heavy wagons such as those in circus parades.

Clydesdale Horses

Special helpers

Dogs make good pets. They make good helpers, too. They are smart and easy to train, so they are often trained to do special jobs.

Guide Dog

Guide dogs help blind people walk without stumbling or bumping into things.

Sheep dogs are trained to help take care of flocks of sheep.

Sheep Dog

In some cold, snowy parts of the world, people travel on big sleds that dogs are trained to pull.

Sled Dogs

When these dogs smell a bird or animal, they point their noses at it to show their master where it is.

Hunting Dogs

Household pets

A pet is an animal friend that lives with you. It may be a big, friendly St. Bernard dog that licks your nose each morning to wake you up. Or maybe it's a fat little hamster that squeaks at you whenever you pass its cage. Whatever it is, remember that it's up to you to give it the care it needs! That's the most important part of owning a pet.

Give a dog or cat food and fresh water each day. Give it a warm, clean place to sleep. Most of all, give it love!

Dog and Cat

Gerbil

Frisky little animals need exercise. If a mouse or gerbil has a wheel like this in its cage, it can run as much as it likes.

Parakeets

Clean your parakeet's cage each day and give it fresh seeds and water. It likes green, leafy vegetables, too.

Hamster

A hamster is clean and friendly. It will eat stale bread, nuts, fruit, and vegetables. Its cage should be kept out of bright light.

Goldfish

A goldfish doesn't need much care. Just keep its water clean and feed it a tiny bit of fish food or breadcrumbs once a day.

In other lands

Many animals we see in zoos are domestic animals of far-off lands.

In India and Southeast Asia, elephants help build roads and clear forests. Camels pull plows and carry people in parts of Africa and Asia. In many parts of the world people keep herds of goats, yaks, camels, llamas, and even reindeer, just as other farmers keep herds of cows or sheep.

In Lapland and parts of the Soviet Union, people keep herds of reindeer, which they train to pull loads.

Reindeer

Asian Elephant

Llamas

In Sri Lanka and some other Asian countries, elephants are trained to lift logs and to help with other heavy labor. In South America, many people use llamas for food, clothing, and to carry things. In some African and Asian countries, many people ride camels and use them for carrying things.

Camels

The great auk is extinct.

Vanishing Animals

You have never seen one of the big, funny-looking birds called dodos. They are extinct. That means there aren't any dodos alive anymore. But 400 years ago, there were many thousands of dodos.

Today, there are many thousands of polar bears, rhinoceroses, and tigers. But they, and many other animals, may soon be extinct, too. Many animals are vanishing. Some are being killed by dirty air and water. Some are being killed by too much hunting. Some are dying because they have no room.

Many people are doing everything they can to keep animals from becoming extinct. But if these people aren't able to save the animals, many of our favorite kinds of animals may soon vanish forever—just like the dodos.

The quagga is extinct.

The dodo is extinct.

People are killing many animals

Almost everywhere in the world more and more wild animals are being killed by people. Many animals are killed for their skins or feathers or horns or tusks. Many animals die when the land where they find their food is covered by factories or airports or highways. Some animals are killed by accident. But unless the killing stops, many kinds of animals will soon be gone from the earth.

These are the skulls of rhinoceroses that were killed just so their horns could be cut off. The horns are sold to people who think they are medicine.

Rhinoceros Skulls

These tusks and skins were taken from hunters who had broken the law by killing too many animals. The hunters wanted to sell the tusks and skins.

Elephant Tusks and Leopard Skins

Many walruses are killed for their tusks. Eskimos carve the tusks into toys to sell. But too many walruses have been killed, so now there are laws to protect them.

Walrus

Green Sea Turtle

The green sea turtles may soon all be gone. They are killed for soup, for oil, and for their skins.

Potomac River Fish

Fish take water into their gills to breathe. If too much waste material is in the water, the fish are killed.

Dirty air and water kill animals

Animals need clean air and water. Many animals cannot breathe air that has lots of smoke and soot in it. Fish and other animals can't live in lakes and rivers that have lots of garbage and waste materials in them. When oil covers the waters of the ocean, many sea animals and birds are killed. And insect sprays kill other animals besides insects.

Water birds can't tell when there is oil in the water. When they try to swim in the oily water, they drown.

Oil Soaked Cormorant

Helping to save animals

Many people work to help keep animals from being killed. For some people, such as game wardens and rangers, helping animals is part of their job. Other people do what they can just because they like animals—and want to save them.

Ducks

Ducks can't find food when rivers and ponds are frozen. These men are breaking the ice so the ducks won't starve.

Hundreds of sea birds were trapped in oily water in the ocean near California. People worked to save as many as they could.

Cleaning Water Birds

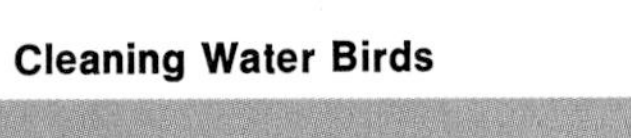

White-Tailed Deer

This deer was trapped by a flood. The game wardens put it to sleep with drugs and took it to safety.

Giraffe

There wasn't enough food where this giraffe lived. It would have starved. But men caught it and moved it by truck to a place where there was plenty of food. Whole herds of animals have been saved this way.

Zoos save some kinds of animals by bringing males and females, such as these oryxes, together. There aren't many of these oryxes left. But if these two have babies and the babies grow up and have more babies, there will soon be more oryxes than there are now. They will be saved from becoming extinct.

Arabian Oryxes

Books to Read

Your school and public library have many interesting books about animals for you to look at and read. You may find these and other books there.

Ages 5 to 8

Ant Cities by Arthur Dorros (Crowell, 1987)
An ant can lift as much as fifty times its own weight. If people could do that, we could each lift a car. This is only one of the many interesting facts that can be found in this book. You'll even learn how to set up your own ant farm.

Beaver at Long Pond by William T. and Lindsey Barrett George (Greenwillow, 1988)
Accompany a beaver as it goes about its nightly activities.

Daytime Animals by Joanna Cole (Knopf, 1985)
This book tells about some animals that are active during the day, and shows life-sized pictures of them. Also look for the companion book, **Nighttime Animals.**

Dinosaur Bones by Aliki (Crowell, 1988)
Find out how, by studying dinosaur bones, scientists learn about dinosaurs and the world they lived in.

Do Not Disturb: The Mysteries of Animal Hibernation and Sleep by Margery Facklam (Little, Brown, 1989)
This book unlocks the secrets of how and why animals hibernate.

Farm Animals by Dorothy Hinshaw Patent (Holiday, 1984)
Wherever you live, on the farm or in the city, you are sure to enjoy this book. The author describes many favorites: cows, goats, pigs, sheep, horses, chickens, guinea hens, turkeys—even cats and dogs.

A First Look at Animals with Horns by Millicent E. Selsam and Joyce Hunt (Walker, 1989)
After reading this book, you will be able to tell many animals by the size and shape of their horns and the direction in which the horns grow.

Ko-hoh: The Call of the Trumpeter Swan by Jay Featherly (Carolrhoda, 1986)
Learn all about this beautiful bird and how it has made a comeback from nearly becoming extinct.

Mammals and Their Milk by Lucia Anderson (Dodd, 1985 1984)
This fascinating book begins by looking at some of the mammals that produce milk. A closer look at what exactly makes up milk follows. There are even simple experiments that will help you see how milk is used to make other products.

Monarch Butterfly by Gail Gibbons (Holiday, 1989)
The monarch butterfly's life cycle and unusual habits are explained with words and bright, bold pictures.

Nature Hide and Seek: Oceans by John Norris Wood (Knopf, 1985)
Lift up the flaps on this book as you try to find the sea creatures that nature has hidden.

Never Kiss an Alligator! by Coleen Stanley Bare (Cobblehill, 1989)
Words and photographs combine to explain many fascinating facts about alligators.

On the Trail of the Fox by Claudia Schnieper (Carolrhoda, 1986)
Unbelievable close-up photographs give you a look at the world of the red fox.

Zoo Day by John Brennan and Leonie Keaney (Carolrhoda, 1989)
Learn about activities that take place at different times of day at a zoo.

Ages 9 and Up

Animal Architects by Donald J. Crump, ed. (National Geographic Society, 1987)
This book answers the question, "Why do animals build?" It also describes the different methods animals use.

Bugs for Dinner? The Eating Habits of Neighborhood Creatures by Sam and Beryl Epstein (Macmillan, 1989)
Join the authors as they explore the eating habits of thirteen creatures that live around you.

The Complete Frog: A Guide for the Very Young Naturalist by Elizabeth Lacey (Lothrop, 1989)
What are the differences between frogs and toads? The author answers this and many other questions about frogs!

Creatures of Long Ago: Dinosaurs by the National Geographic Society Staff (National Geographic Society, 1989)
This pop-up book explains many interesting facts about the giant reptiles that ruled the earth for millions of years.

The Crocodile and the Crane: Surviving in a Crowded World by Judy Cutchins and Ginny Johnston (Morrow, 1986)
The crocodile, the crane, and four other endangered species of animals are covered in this book.

The Digging Badger by Kathryn A. Minta (Putnam, 1985)
The author describes field studies on badgers in this informative book.

Inside the Burrow: The Life of the Golden Hamster by Heiderose and Andreas Fischer-Nagel (Carolrhoda, 1986)
This book tells all about hamsters both in the wild and in captivity and explains how to care for them.

Peeping in the Shell: A Whooping Crane Is Hatched by Faith McNulty (Crowell, 1986)
This is the true story of how Tex, a whooping crane, hatches her egg.

Snakes by Sylvia A. Johnson (Lerner, 1986)
Did you ever wonder how snakes are able to move through the water? The author of this informative book explains how they do this and much, much more.

Wolf Pack: Tracking Wolves in the Wild by Sylvia Johnson and Alice Aamodt (Lerner, 1987)
If you have a pet dog at home, you may be interested to find out that your dog's ancestors were wolves.

The World of Fishes by Hiroshi Takeuchi (Raintree, 1986)
This book explores the unusual fish of the coral reefs and the deep.

New Words

Some of the words you have met in this book may be new to you. Many of them are words you'll meet again, so they are good words to know. Some are the names of animals. Here are some of these words. Next to each word you are shown how to say it: **algae** (AL jee). The part shown in capital letters is said a little more loudly than the rest of the word. Under each word, the meaning is given in a complete sentence.

ajolote (ah hoh LOH tay)
An ajolote is a two-legged lizard with a wormlike body.

algae (AL jee)
Algae are plants that live mainly in water and make their own food.

amphibian (am FIHB ee uhn)
An amphibian is an animal that lives in water and breathes with gills when it is a baby. It lives on land and breathes with lungs when it is an adult. Frogs and toads are amphibians.

anaconda (an uh KAHN duh)
The anaconda is the largest South American snake. It lives near water and eats mainly birds and small animals.

Anglaspis (an GLAS pihs)
The Anglaspis was a jawless fish that lived in the sea millions of years ago.

Apatosaurus (ap uh toh SAWR uhs)
An Apatosaurus was a gigantic, plant-eating dinosaur with four elephantlike legs, a long neck, and a long tail.

aphid (AY fihd)
An aphid is a tiny insect that feeds by sucking juices from plants and trees.

arachnid (uh RAK nihd)
An arachnid is an insectlike animal with no feelers or wings. It has four pairs of jointed legs. Spiders and daddy-longlegs are arachnids.

Archaeopteryx (ahr kee AHP tuhr ihks)
The Archaeopteryx was a crow-sized bird that lived millions of years ago. It had claws on its wings, and teeth.

arthropod (AHR thruh pahd)
An arthropod is an animal with jointed legs and an outside shell. Insects, spiders, and shrimps are all arthropods.

bacteria (bak TIHR ee uh)
Bacteria are tiny creatures that can be seen only with a microscope. They may be oval, rod-shaped, or spiral.

biologist (by AHL uh jihst)
A biologist is a person who studies living things in all their forms.

Birkenia (buhr KEE nee uh)
A Birkenia was a small, jawless fish that lived in the sea millions of years ago.

bombardier beetle (bahm buhr DIHR BEE tuhl)
A bombardier beetle is a ground insect. It makes a popping sound and lets off a bad-smelling gas when it is in danger.

brachiopod (BRAK ee uh pahd)
A brachiopod is a shellfish with two differently shaped shells.

Brachiosaurus (brak ee uh SAWR uhs)
A Brachiosaurus was one of the largest of all dinosaurs. It had a huge body and a short tail.

Brontosaurus (brahn tuh SAWR uhs)
Brontosaurus is another name for an Apatosaurus. The name means "thunder lizard."

caecilian (see SIHL ee uhn)
A caecilian is an animal that looks like a worm. It is related to frogs and toads.

centipede (SEHN tuh peed)
A centipede is a small wormlike animal whose body is divided into many parts. Each part has a pair of thin legs attached.

Cephalaspis (sehf uh LAS pihs)
A Cephalaspis was a kind of fish that lived millions of years ago. It had a large bony shield attached to its head.

chaffinch (CHAF ihnch)
A chaffinch is a small European songbird.

chameleon (kuh MEE lee uhn)
A chameleon is a lizard. It can change its color to blend in with its surroundings.

cicada (suh KAY duh)
A cicada is an insect with four thin wings. The male cicada makes a buzzing sound in hot, dry weather.

Coccosteus (kuh KAHS tee uhs)
A Coccosteus was a jawless, armored fish that lived in the sea long ago.

Coelophysis (see LAHF uh sihs)
A Coelophysis was one of the first dinosaurs. It had a long neck and a long tail. It ran on its hind legs.

conch (kahngk)
A conch is a large, heavy, sea snail that has a twisty, cone-shaped shell.

crustacean (kruhs TAY shuhn)
A crustacean is a kind of animal that has a shell-covered body and many jointed legs. Most crustaceans live in or near water. Crabs, lobsters, and shrimps are crustaceans.

diatom (DY uh tahm)
A diatom is a tiny water plant.

Dimetrodon (dy MEH truh dahn)
The Dimetrodon was a reptile that lived millions of years ago. It had a large fin on its back.

dinosaur (DY nuh sawr)
A dinosaur is any one of two groups of reptiles that lived millions of years ago.

dolphin (DAHL fihn)
A dolphin is a sea mammal that belongs to the whale family. It is smaller than a whale.

echidna (ih KIHD nuh)
An echidna, also called a spiny anteater, is a small mammal. It has a flattened body that is covered with coarse hair and sharp spines.

elephant-nose mormyrid (EHL uh fuhnt-nohz mawr MY rihd)
An elephant-nose mormyrid is a fresh-water fish that lives in Africa.

Eohippus (ee oh HIHP uhs)
The Eohippus was the ancestor of the horse. It was a small animal about 10 to 20 inches high.

gerbil (JUR buhl)
A gerbil is a furry, mouselike animal with a long tail. It lives in the dry, sandy parts of Africa and Asia.

gnu (noo)
Gnu is another name for a wildebeest. It is a large animal that lives in Africa.

great auk (grayt awk)
The great auk was a bird that lived on the coasts of the North Atlantic Ocean. There are no great auks alive today.

grebe (greeb)
A grebe is a bird that dives to get fish. It has a flattened body covered with waterproof feathers.

hedgehog (HEHJ hahg)
A hedgehog is a small, insect-eating animal. It has a long nose, a short tail, and stiff, pointed growths, called spines, on its back.

hibernation (hy buhr NAY shuhn)
Hibernation is a deep sleep that some animals take during the winter. Badgers, ground squirrels, marmots, and some other animals hibernate.

Ichthyostega (ihk thee AHS tee guh)
The Ichthyostega was the first amphibian. It looked like a fish with legs. It lived millions of years ago.

iguanid (ih GWAH nihd)
An iguanid is a kind of lizard. It belongs to the same family as the iguana, the horned toad, and the pine lizard.

jaguar (JAG wahr)
A jaguar is a large, wild cat. It has dark yellow fur with black or brown spots.

jewel cichlid (JOO uhl SIHK lihd)
A jewel cichlid is a small, bright-colored freshwater fish. It has spiny fins and jewellike spots of color on its sides.

kiwi (KEE wee)
A kiwi is a shaggy-feathered bird about as big as a chicken. It has no tail and cannot fly because its wings are too small.

koala (koh AH luh)
A koala is a small animal that lives in Australia. It looks somewhat like a teddy bear.

kudu (KOO doo)
A kudu is a big African antelope. It lives in the grassy parts of the Sahara.

macaw (muh KAW)
A macaw is a long-tailed, brightly colored parrot.

millipede (MIHL uh peed)
A millipede is a wormlike animal with many thin legs.

Moeritherium (mihr uh THIHR ee uhm)
The Moeritherium was a small animal that lived millions of years ago in Egypt. It was the ancestor of the elephant.

mosquito (muh SKEE toh)
Mosquito is the Spanish word for *little fly*. The female mosquito has mouthparts that can stab the skin of animals and humans and draw blood. The itching and swelling called a mosquito bite is caused by the mosquito's saliva.

naturalist (NACH uhr uh lihst)
A naturalist studies plants and animals in the places where they live.

nuthatch (NUHT hach)
A nuthatch is a small, climbing bird that lives mostly in trees.

onychophoran (ahn uh koh FAWR uhn)
An onychophoran is a small, wormlike animal. It has thick, short legs attached to the many parts of its body.

orangutan (oh RANG u tan)
An orangutan is a large, reddish-brown ape. It has long, strong arms.

oryx (AWR ihks)
An oryx is an African antelope.

pangolin (pang GOH luhn)
A pangolin is a mammal that has scales on its body. It looks like a combination of an anteater and an armadillo.

platypus (PLAT uh puhs)
A platypus is an egg-laying mammal. Its bill is shaped like a duck's bill.

porpoise (PAWR puhs)
A porpoise is a small mammal that belongs to the whale family. It is sometimes mistaken for a dolphin.

psychologist (sy KAHL uh jihst)
A psychologist is a person who is trained to understand the mind and its activities.

Pteranodon (tehr AN uh dahn)
The Pteranodon was a flying reptile about the size of a turkey. It lived millions of years ago.

Pterichthyodes (tuh rihk thee OH deez)
The Pterichthyodes was a kind of fish that lived millions of years ago. Its head and back were protected by bony armor.

Pterygotus (tehr uh GOH tuhs)
The Pterygotus was a lobsterlike animal. It lived millions of years ago.

quagga (KWAHG uh)
The quagga was a zebra that had stripes on the front part of its body only. It lived in South Africa. There are no quaggas any more. They are extinct.

Rhamphorhynchus (ram fuh RIHN kuhs)
The Rhamphorhynchus was a flying reptile that lived long ago. It had a long, paddlelike tail, and long, sharp teeth.

scallop (SKAHL uhp)
A scallop is a shellfish. It belongs to the same family as the oyster.

sea anemone (see uh NEHM uh nee)
A sea anemone is a bright-colored sea animal that looks like the flower from which it gets its name. It belongs to the same family as the jellyfish and the coral.

spore (spawr)
A spore is a tiny kind of seed. Molds and mushrooms grow from spores.

sturgeon (STUR juhn)
A sturgeon is a large fish with a long body. Its eggs are used to make caviar.

Stylonurus (sty LAHN uh ruhs)
The Stylonurus was a prehistoric sea animal with a hard shell and many jointed legs.

termite (TUR myt)
A termite is an insect. Sometimes called white ants, termites live in colonies.

Thelodus (THEHL uh duhs)
A Thelodus was a bony-armored fish that lived in the sea millions of years ago.

tortoise (TAWR tuhs)
A tortoise is a turtle that lives on land.

Tremataspis (tree muh TAS pihs)
The Tremataspis was a jawless, bony-armored fish that lived long ago.

Triassochelys (try ahs oh KEHL eez)
The Triassochelys was a turtle that lived millions of years ago. It was much like today's turtle, but it could not pull its head and legs all the way into its shell.

Triceratops (try SEHR uh tahps)
The Triceratops was a dinosaur that lived in the western part of North America millions of years ago. It had a big head with a horn over each eye and on its nose.

trilobite (TRY loh byt)
A trilobite was a small, shell-covered, prehistoric sea animal with feelers and many legs. Its shell was divided into three sections or lobes. Its name means *three lobes.* It breathed through gills in its legs.

tuatara (too uh TAH ruh)
The tuatara is a large reptile that lives in New Zealand.

turbot (TUR buht)
A turbot is a large, round, flatfish. It swims on its side, and its two eyes are on the left side of its head.

Tyrannosaurus (ty ran uh SAWR uhs)
The Tyrannosaurus was a huge, meat-eating dinosaur. It walked upright on its two hind legs.

ultraviolet (uhl truh VY uh liht)
Ultraviolet is a color that some animals can see. It is invisible to people.

wildebeest (WIHL duh beest)
A wildebeest is a large animal that lives in Africa. It has a big head with long, curved horns, skinny legs, and a long tail. It is also known as a gnu (noo).

wrasse (ras)
A wrasse is a bright-colored fish with spiny fins. It has thick lips and strong teeth. It lives in warm seas.

zoologist (zoh AHL uh jihst)
A zoologist is a person who studies animal life.

zoology (zoh AHL uh jee)
Zoology is the study of animal life.

Illustration acknowledgments

The publishers of *Childcraft* gratefully acknowledge the following artists, photographers, publishers, agencies, and corporations for illustrations in this volume. Page numbers refer to two-page spreads. The words *"(left)," "(center)," "(top)," "(bottom),"* and *"(right)"* indicate position on the spread. All illustrations are the exclusive property of the publishers of *Childcraft* unless names are marked with an asterisk (*).

1: *(top left)* Childcraft photo; Treat Davidson, NAS *; *(center left)* Warren Garst *; *(center right)* Guy Tudor; *(bottom left)* Harry McNaught; *(bottom right)* Walter Linsenmaier
4-5: Eraldo Carugati and George Lopac
6-7: Jane Burton, Bruce Coleman Ltd. *; Laura D'Argo
8-9: *(top left)* Nelson Medina, Photo Researchers *, *(center left)* R. A. Mendez, Photo Trends *; *(bottom left)* Russ Kinne, Photo Researchers *; Allan Roberts *; *(center right)* Warren Garst, Tom Stack & Associates *
10-11: *(top left)* Appel Color Photography *; *(bottom left)* Walter Dawn *; *(top right)* Ralph Buchsbaum *; *(bottom right)* E. R. Degginger *
12-13: *(top left)* Rohm & Hass Company *; *(bottom left)* Francisco Erize, Bruce Coleman Ltd. *; *(right)* Walter Chandoha
14-15: *(left)* William Bridge, Tom Stack & Associates *; *(top right)* Warren Garst, Tom Stack & Associates *; *(bottom right)* Russ Kinne, Photo Researchers *
16-17: *(top left)* Warren Garst *; *(center left)* Warren Garst *; *(bottom left)* © Michael and Barbara Reed, Animals Animals *; *(top right)* © Diana Rogers, Bruce Coleman Inc. *; *(center right)* Carleton Ray, Photo Researchers *; *(bottom right)* Zig Leszczynski, Animals Animals *
18-19: *(top left)* Walter Rohdich, APF *; *(center left)* Anthony Mercieca, NAS *, Glen Sherwood *; *(bottom left)* Nelson Medina, Burton McNeely Photography *; *(top right)* Lars Christiansen, APF *; *(bottom right)* Dan Gibson, Miller Services *
20-21: *(top left)* R. F. Head, NAS *; *(bottom left)* Robert Hermes, APF *; *(top right)* Stephen Collins, Photo Researchers *; *(bottom right)* Warren Garst *, Jane Burton, Photo Researchers *
22-23: *(top left)* Warren Garst *; *(bottom left)* Tom McHugh, Photo Researchers *; *(top right)* © J. A. L. Cooke, Oxford Scientific Films from Animals Animals *; *(center right)* Noble Proctor, Photo Researchers *; *(bottom right)* C. E. Mohr, NAS *
24-25: M. P. L. Fogden, Adrian Davies, Dieter and Mary Plage, Bruce Coleman Ltd. *
26-27: Peter Snowball
28-29: Norman Weaver
30-31: *(left)* Laura D'Argo; *(right)* G. J. Chafaris *
32-33: *(left)* J. M. Conrader *; *(right)* George P. Miller, Black Star *
34-35: *(left)* John Cancalosi, Tom Stack & Associates *; *(center top)* Roberta Polfus; *(center left)* Jen and Des Bartlett, Bruce Coleman Inc. *; *(right)* Grant Thomson, APF *; *(bottom right)* Leonard Lee Rue III, Bruce Coleman Ltd. *
36-37: *(left)* Don Moss: *(right)* J. Van Wormer, Bruce Coleman, Inc. *
38-39: *(left)* Norman Weaver; *(right)* Zefa Picture Library *
40-41: *(left)* Bernhard Grzimek, Okapia *; *(right)* Norman Weaver
42-43: *(left)* Norman Weaver; *(top right)* Tom McHugh, Photo Researchers *; *(center right)* Eric Hosking *; *(bottom right)* James Loy, TSW/Click/Chicago *
44-45: Betty Fraser
46-47: *(left)* Zig Leszczynski, Animals Animals *; *(right)* © Carl R. Sams II *
48-49: *(top left)* © Carl R. Sams II *; *(bottom left)* Tom Edwards, Animals Animals *; *(right)* J. Van Wormer, Bruce Coleman, Inc. *
50-51: Guy Tudor
52-53: *(left)* Laura D'Argo; *(right)* Russ Kinne, Photo Researchers *
54-55: Arthur Twomey, Photo Researchers *
56-57: *(left)* G. Ronald Austing *; *(right)* Guy Tudor
58-59: *(left)* © VIREO *; *(top right)* G. Ronald Austing, NAS *
60-61: *(top left)* G. Ronald Austing *; *(bottom left)* Perry Covington, Tom Stack & Associates *; *(top right)* R. F. Head, NAS *; John C. Schmid, Photo Researchers *; *(bottom right)* Bradley Smith, Photo Researchers *; Sandy Sprunt, NAS *; Art: Betty Fraser
62-63: *(left and top right)* Sheila Galbraith, B. L. Kearley Ltd.; *(center right)* © S. Nielsen, DRK Photo *
64-67: Glen Sherwood *
68-69: Norman Weaver
70-71: *(left)* Laura D'Argo; Russ Kinne, Photo Researchers *
72-73: Jane Burton, Bruce Coleman Ltd. *
74-75: *(left)* Marineland of Florida *; *(right)* Laurence Perkins *
76-77: *(top)* Zig Leszczynski, Animals Animals *; *(bottom)* Norman Weaver
78-79: *(left top)* Alain Compost, Bruce Coleman Ltd. *; *(left bottom)* Annabel Milne; *(right)* Norman Weaver
80-81: *(left)* © Doug Perrine, DRK *; *(bottom right)* Ron Church *
82-83: Harry McNaught
84-85: *(left)* Laura D'Argo; *(right)* G. Ronald Austing *
86-87: Alan Male, Linden Artists Ltd.
88-89: Harry McNaught
90-91: *(left)* Leonard Lee Rue, Bruce Coleman Ltd *; *(right)* E. R. Degginger, Animals Animals *
92-93: © John Visser, Bruce Coleman, Inc. *
94-95: *(left)* C. B. and D. W. Firth, Bruce Coleman Ltd. *; *(right)* Robert E. Lunt, APF *
96-99: Harry McNaught
100-101: *(left)* Laura D'Argo; *(right)* Walter Rohdich, APF *
102-103: *(top left and center left)* G. Ronald Austing *; *(bottom left)* W. Mahoney, Shostal *; *(top right)* Leonard Lee Rue III, APF *; *(bottom right)* E. R. Degginger *
104-105: *(left)* George Porter, NAS *; *(right)* Jane Burton, Bruce Coleman Ltd. *
106-107: Harry McNaught
108-109: *(top left)* S. C. Bisserot, Photo Researchers *; *(center left and bottom left)* Jane Burton, Photo Researchers *; *(top right)* James H. Keller * *(bottom right)* Jane Burton, Photo Researchers *
110-111: Walter Linsenmaier
112-113: *(top left)* Betty Fraser; *(bottom left)* Lia Munson *; *(top right)* A. W. Cooper, Photo Researchers *; *(bottom right)* Hermann Eisenbeiss, Photo Researchers *
114-115: *(top left)* Otto W. Wehrle, Photo Researchers *; *(bottom left)* John H. Gerard, NAS *; *(top right)* Richard Parker, DPI *; *(bottom right)* Betty Fraser
116-117: *(left)* Walter Linsenmaier; *(top right)* Walter Dawn *; *(bottom right)* Betty Fraser
118-119: *(left)* W. Harstrick, Wisniewski, W. Schmidt, Zefa Picture Library *; *(right)* Hans Reinhard, Bruce Coleman Ltd. *
120-121: *(left)* Alexander B. Klots *, S. C. Bisserot, Bruce Coleman Ltd. *; *(right)* Alexander B. Klots *, S. C. Bisserot, Bruce Coleman Ltd.
122-123: Edward S. Ross *
124-125: *(left)* Jane Burton, Bruce Coleman Ltd. *; *(center and bottom right)* Ross E. Hutchins *
126-127: *(top left)* Treat Davidson, NAS *; *(center left)* Jerome Wexler Photo Researchers *; *(bottom left)* Phillippe Scott, Photo Researchers *; *(top right)* Larry West, NAS *; *(bottom right)* Arthur W. Ambler, NAS *
128-129: *(left) Walter Linsenmaier; (top right)* Walter Linsenmaier; *(bottom right)* Walter Dawn *
130-133: Walter Linsenmaier
134-135: Jane Burton, Bruce Coleman Ltd. *; Zefa Picture Library *
136-137: *(left and right)* Douglas Faulkner *
138-139: *(top left)* George Lower *; *(bottom left)* Terry Shaw, APF *; *(right)* Darrell Ward, Tom Stack & Associates *
140-141: D. P. Wilson, F.R.P.S., Marine Biological Laboratory, Plymouth, England *
142-143: *(top left)* Laura D'Argo; *(bottom)* Walter Linsenmaier
144-145: *(top left)* N. J. Berrill *; *(bottom left)* Russ Kinne, Photo Researchers *; *(top right)* Allan Power, Bruce Coleman Ltd. *; *(bottom right)* B. Bartram Cadbury, NAS *

146-147: Norman Weaver
148-149: *(top)* Jane P. Downton, Tom Stack & Associates *; *(bottom)* Lia Munson *, Erick Hosking *
150-151: Lilo Hess, Three Lions *
152-153: *(left)* Joe McDonald, Animals Animals *; *(right)* John Wallis, Bruce Coleman Ltd. *
154-155: *(left)* Gerald Cubitt, Bruce Coleman Ltd. *; *(right)* C. B. and D. W. Firth, Bruce Coleman Ltd. *; © John Eastcott and Yva Momatiuk, DRK *
156-157: Norman Myers, Bruce Coleman Inc. *
158-159: James Simon, Photo Researchers *
160-161: Norman Weaver
162-163: *(left)* Animals Animals *; *(right)* Laura D'Argo
164-165: *(left)* © George J. Sanker, DRK *; *(top right)* De Wys, Inc. *; *(bottom right)* © Stephen J. Krasemann, DRK *
166-167: *(top right)* Leonard Lee Rue, Shostal *; *(bottom right)* Walter Dawn *
168-169: Tom Myers *
170-171: *(top)* Norman Myers, Photo Researchers *; *(bottom)* Douglas Faulkner *
172-173: *(left)* © George Holton, Photo Researchers *; *(right)* Norman Weaver
174-175: Norman Weaver
176-177: Stefan Meyers, Ardea *
178-179: Alex Ebel
180-181: *(top left)* Horst Bielfeld, NAS *; *(bottom left)* Jane Burton, Bruce Coleman Ltd. *; *(right)* M. W. F. Tweedle, NAS *
182-183: *(left)* Kim Taylor, Bruce Coleman Ltd. *; *(right)* Larry Frederick
184-185: *(top left)* Karl Maslowski *; *(bottom left)* Louis Quitt, Photo Researchers *; *(top right)* Raymond A. Mendez, Photo Trends *
186-187: *(left)* Alex Ebel; *(right)* John Shaw, Bruce Coleman Ltd. *
188-189: John Markham, Bruce Coleman Ltd. *
190-191: *(left)* Willis Peterson *; *(right)* Carleton Ray, Photo Researchers *
192-193: *(left)* E. R. Degginger *; *(right)* Norman Myers, Photo Researchers *
194-195: *(left)* Douglas Baglin Photography, Pty., Ltd., NAS *; *(right)* Russ Kinne, Photo Researchers *
196-197: *(left)* Van Nostrand Photo, NAS *; *(right)* Leonard Lee Rue, III, NAS *
198-199: *(left)* John Moyer, NAS *; *(right)* Yoshi Miyake
200-201: *(top left)* Larry Frederick; *(bottom left and right)* Betty Fraser
202-203: Harry McNaught
204-205: H. Doering, APF *
206-207: © E. E. Kingsley, Photo Researchers *
208-209: Harry McNaught
210-211: *(left)* © Ray Richardson, Animals Animals *; *(right)* Russ Kinne, Photo Researchers *
212-213: *(right)* G. Ronald Austing, NAS *
214-215: Harry McNaught
216-217: Syd Greenberg, Photo Researchers *
218-219: *(left)* Jan Wills; *(right top)* © Phil Savoie, Bruce Coleman, Inc. *; *(right center)* Larry Frederick
220-221: Alex Ebel
222-223: *(left)* Mas Nakagawa: *(right)* Alex Ebel
224-225: *(left)* Alex Ebel; *(right)* Mas Nakagawa
226-227: *(left)* Mas Nakagawa; *(right)* Alex Ebel
228-235: Alex Ebel
236-237: Colin Newman
238-239: *(top)* Russ Kinne, Photo Researchers *; *(bottom)* Laurence Pringle, NAS *
240-243: Alex Ebel
244-245: Kimmerle Milnazik
246-247: *(top left)* Alan Band Associates *; *(bottom left) Childcraft* photo by Flip Schulke, Black Star; *(right) Childcraft* photos by Flip Schulke, Black Star
248-251: *Childcraft* photos by Flip Schulke, Black Star
252-253: *(top left)* Donald S. Sade, Van Cleve Photography *; *(center left)* Glen Sherwood *; *(bottom left)* George Holton, Photo Researchers *; *(top and bottom right)* Flip Schulke, Black Star *
254-255: *(left)* Dr. Ronald Cohn, The Gorilla Foundation *; *(top right)* Brenda Anderson *; *(bottom right)* Harry Redl, Black Star *
256-257: *(top left)* Terrence Spencer, Black Star *; *(bottom left)* © Tony Dawson; *(right)* Patricia Cauldfield, Photo Researchers *
258-259: *(left)* Dan Bernstein, Photo Researchers *; *(center left)* Fritz Prenzel, Animals Animals *
260-261: *(top left) Childcraft* photo by Virginia Eckelberry; *(bottom left) Childcraft* photo by Bernard Photographers; *(right)* reproduction of painting "Bobwhite" by Don Richard Eckelberry © Frame House Gallery, Louisville, Ky. *
262-263: *(top left)* Robert J. Lee; *(bottom)* Robert J. Lee; Laura D'Argo; *(right)* Robert J. Lee
264-265: *(left)* H. Armstrong Roberts *; *(right)* Jerry Frank, DPI *
266-267: *(top left)* Walter Chandoha *; *(bottom left)* © Susan Jones, Animals Animals *; *(center right)* Grant Heilman *; *(bottom right)* Grant Heilman
268-269: *(top left and center left)* Herb and Dorothy McLaughlin *; *(bottom left)* Leonard Lee Rue III, Animals Animals *
270-271: *(left)* A. M. Wettach *; *(top right)* Grant Heilman *; *(bottom right)* Bart Jarner
272-273: *(top left) Childcraft* photo; *(bottom left)* Roland and Sabrina Michaud, Rapho Guillumette *; *(right)* George Lopac
274-275: *(top left)* Frank Siteman from Marilyn Gartman *; *(bottom left)* Bart Jarner; *(top right)* © Mickey Gibson, Animals Animals *; *(center right)* Miller Services *; *(bottom right)* Mickey Gibson, Animals Animals *
276-277: *(left)* Walter Chandoha *; *(center left)* Sybil Shackman, Monkmeyer *; (top right) Stephen Collins, NAS *; *(center right)* Joe Monroe, Photo Researchers *; *(bottom right)* Treat Davidson, NAS *
278-279: *(left)* © Dan Budnik, Woodfin Camp, Inc. *; *(top right)* © Mickey Gibson, Animals Animals *; *(center right)* Miller Services *; *(bottom right)* © Mickey Gibson, Animals Animals *
280-281: Peter Barrett
282-283: *(top left)* Graham Young, Photo Trends *; *(bottom left)* Mark N. Boulton, NAS *; *(top right)* Georg Gerster, Rapho Guillumette *; *(bottom right) Childcraft* photo by Ray Halin
284-285: *(left) Childcraft* photo by Weston Kemp: *(right)* John Neel, Tom Stack & Associates *
286-287: *(top left)* Publix Pictorial *; *(bottom left)* Al Satterwhite, Camera 5 *, Cyril Maitland, Camera 5 *; *(top right and bottom)* Lynn Pelham, Rapho Guillumette *
288: *(top left)* von Meiss-Teuffen, Photo Researchers *; *(bottom left)* Bradley Smith, Photo Researchers *

Cover: Elizabeth Miles

Index

This index is an alphabetical list of the important topics covered in this book. It will help you find information given in both words *and* pictures. To help you understand what an entry means, there is often a helping word in parentheses. For example, **sole** (fish). If there is information in both words and pictures, you will see the words *(with pictures)* after the page number. If there is *only* a picture, you will see the word *(picture)* after the page number. If you do not find what you want in this index, please go to the General Index in Volume 15, which is a key to all of the books.